D1559408

PORPHYRY'S
C AGAINST THE
HRISTIANS

THE LITERARY REMAINS

Edited and Translated with an
Introduction and Epilogue by

R. Joseph Hoffmann,
Oxford University

Prometheus Books
59 John Glenn Drive
Amherst, New York 14228-2197

Published 1994 by Prometheus Books

98 97 96 95 94   5 4 3 2 1

Library of Congress Cataloging-in-Publication Data

Porphyry, ca. 234–ca. 305.
    [Against the Christians. English]
    Porphyry's Against the Christians : the literary remains /
edited and translated with an introduction and epilogue by
R. Joseph Hoffmann.
        p.   cm.
    Includes bibliographical references.
    ISBN 0-87975-889-9 (alk. paper)
    1. Christianity—Controversial literature—Early works to
1800. 2. Christianity—Early church, ca. 30–600—Sources.
I. Hoffmann, R. Joseph. II. Title. III. Title: Against the
Christians.
BR160.3.P6713   1994
230—dc20   94-6779
                                                               CIP

Printed in the United States of America on acid-free paper.

Contents

Introduction

Persecution as Context

In the year 312 Christianity gained the right to permanent existence as a religion of the Roman empire. By this time it was nearly three centuries old. Christian mythography and the lives of the saints used to insist that the way to legality had been an uphill struggle, guided by providence, perhaps, but strewn with the bodies of the martyrs, the church's "seed," as Tertullian boasted in his *Apology*. "The more we are mown down by you pagans, the more we grow." Still, there was something ominously correct in Tertullian's boast. At the end of the second century, when both Tertullian and the pagan philosopher Celsus were active in their campaigns for and against the church, the pagan philosopher could say with Grouchoesque humor, "If all men wanted to be Christians, the Christians would not want them."

Only a decade or so later, Tertullian could argue with equal conviction that the church had grown by such bursts that, "If the emperor were to exterminate the Christians he would find himself without an empire to rule."

The use of hyperbole to win converts did not begin with twentieth-century evangelism; it was a feature of the quarrel between pagan culture and Christian teaching from its beginning, and a trademark of the Greek and Latin rhetoric in which the argument was conducted.

Yet things changed quickly for the Christians. Martyrs

there were, and fickle emperors ranging from Philip the Arab to Aurelian to Diocletian, men who could not make up their minds, or changed them after they had. In 248, Celsus' literary opponent, Origen, wrote: "Though [we lack] workers to bring in the harvest of souls, there is a harvest nevertheless: men and women brought in upon God's threshing floor, the churches. which are everywhere" (*Contra Celsum* 3.9). The boast that a *plethos* (a multitude) of people had entered the church—a boast for Tertullian, an outrage to Celsus and his intellectual compadres, and later also for Porphyry—set off an alarm heard throughout the Roman empire.

The third century was not just an age of persecution; it was the only century in which persecution affected Christians generally. The empire itself was in the throes of a power struggle and crisis of confidence, beginning with Decius in February of 250, and extending through the reigns of Valerian (257-260) and Diocletian (284-305). With periods of remission, the effort to control the growth of the Christian movement lasted from 250 until 284. Then, on 23 February 303, at the height of his power, Diocletian outlawed Christianity. Even after his abdication in 305, persecution continued in the east for seven more years under Galerius and Maximinus Daia.

But persecution is a slippery term in the annals of the early church. An older generation of church historians, using the martyrologies and writings of the church fathers as their sources, believed that the era from Nero to Constantine was one of almost unremitting slaughter of professing Christians. Their opinion was enfeebled somewhat by the certainty that the Romans could have tried a "final solution" to the Christian problem much earlier, if they had wanted, and the fact that along with boasting of their many martyrs, church writers like Origen also bragged that rich folk, high officials, elegant ladies and *illuminati* were entering the church in great numbers. The pagan writers tried to counter this trend in their insistence that Christianity was really a religion for the lazy, the ignorant and superstitious, and the lowborn—"women, yokels and children," Celsus had sneered. But the ploy was ineffective. Diocletian's persecutions revealed that Christianity had crept into the emperor's bedroom: his wife, his daughter, their servants, the treasury official Audactus, the eunuch Dorotheus, even the director of the purple dye factory in Tyre, were Christians or Christian sympathizers. Insulting the new converts did not stop the process of conversion. The political solution of the third century, therefore, was an attempt to scare people off— to make being a Christian an expensive proposition. Persecution was the strong-arm alternative to failed polemical tactics by the likes of Celsus, Porphyry and Hierocles. It was a last-gasp attempt to save the old religious order from the muddled legalism of Christian moral teaching, which had been carelessly satirized as bacchic frenzy. Perhaps even by Celsus' day (since he barely alludes to Christian immorality) nobody believed the gossip. Christian and pagan neighbors in fourth-century Damascus winked at each other and giggled behind their hands when a zealous magistrate rounded up a gaggle of prostitutes from the city market and forced them into signing an admission that they were "Christian whores."

How were Christian persecuted? Almost on the eve of persecution, the Christian writer Origen said with pride that "we [Christians] have enjoyed peace for a long time now." But Origen also saw clouds on the horizon. Political instability and military disaster threatened; economic times were hard. Duty (*pietas*) required that loyal Romans should stand behind the traditions and honor the cults that had so far ensured their greatness. From the standpoint of staunch pagans and the Roman intellectual class, the past two generations had been characterized by slippage and erosion, a watering down of tradition. The ranks had to be closed.

In 250 Decius decreed simply that Christians would be required to sacrifice to the gods of Rome by offering wine and eating sacrificial meat. Those who refused would be sentenced to death. To avoid this punishment, well-to-do Christians seem to have given up the new religion in substantial numbers, becoming in the eyes of the faithful "apostates," a new designation derived from the Greek work for revolt. The apostates also numbered many bishops, including the bishop of the important region of Smyrna, as well as Jewish Christians who rejoined the synagogue, as Judaism was not encompassed in the Decian order. Subsequently the church was racked with confusion about what to do with those Christians who had lapsed from the faith in time of trouble but who wished to reenter the church once the troubles had passed—the so-called *lapsi*. Augustine would find himself still dealing with the problem in fifth-century Africa. The Christian sacraments of baptism and (to a degree) the eucharist were reconceived against the political background of apostate priests and bishops: When was a sacrament not a sacrament? When it had been "performed" by a traitor to the cause, argued some. The effects of persecution thus worked themselves out in specific ways, even in the doctrine of the church.

In the reign of Valerian (253–260) the focus shifted from the practice of the Christian faith to the church's ownership of property—a cause of concern to pagan conservatives who had come to associate the rise of Christianity with the death of the old order. There is plenty to suggest that Christians in the middle of the third century had become self-confident and even ostentatious about the practice of their faith. In Nicomedia, the eastern capital of the empire, "the Christian church stood tall, visible from the palace" (Lactantius, *On the Death of the Persecutors* 12; Cyprian, *Epistle* 80.2). With money and property, Roman-style, came acceptability; the Christians were following the pattern of pagan philanthropists, endowing churches where previously they would have endowed shrines to the state gods. They were becoming, in a word, respectable.

In August 257, Valerian targeted the wealth of the clergy and in 258 the riches of prominent Christian lay persons. The tactic was obviously intended to make upper-crust Romans think twice before throwing their wealth in the direction of the "beggar priests" as Porphyry called them, and making themselves wards of the *nouveaux riches* lords of the church. In a society where well-being and wealth were nothing to be ashamed of, the Christian emphasis on poverty and suffering seemed to be less incomprehensible than merely foolish, a scam run by church officials at the expense of gullible, religion-hungry *honestiores*. The Valerian edict also included a provision that "members of Caesar's household who have confessed or confess [to being Christians] should be sent in chains as slaves to work on Caesar's farms" (Cyprian, Epistle 80.1), while senators and men of rank should first lose their property and, only if they persisted, their heads.

The proceedings could be summary or drawn out. The record for short hearings seems to belong to the Roman governor of Spain in his interrogation of a bishop:

"Are you a bishop?"
"I am."
"You mean you *were*." (*Acts of Fructuosus* 2)

In 258, St. Cyprian, the great bishop of Carthage in North Africa, was executed after a lengthy interrogation by Galerius Maximus. The case is an interesting one from the standpoint of pagan-Christian relations. Cyprian had been pestered by a second-rate philosopher named Demetrian for a number of years. Demetrian argued—as many had before and many would afterward—that Christianity was responsible for the calamities of the empire, an assessment which Tertullian ridicules as early as the year 198. In the language of the "moral majority" of his day, Demetrian insisted that if only the Christians would pay due reverence to the state cults and to the person of the emperor, peace and prosperity would return. When he was finally goaded to respond, Cyprian's answer was an oracle of doom, a longwinded paraphrase of Lucretius (cf. *De rerum natura* 2.1105f.) asserting that the world was in the throes of decay:

> The farmer fails and languishes in the fields, the sailor at sea, the soldier at camp. Honesty fails in the marketplace; justice in the courts; love from friendship; skill from the arts; discipline from conduct. . . . It is a sentence passed upon the world, it is God's law, that as things rose, so they should fall; as they waxed, so should they grow old. . . . And when they become weak and little, they die. (Cyprian, *To Demetrian* 3)

This "philosophical apocalypse" was nothing that Roman ears would have liked. For the Christians to quote from their own eccentric scriptures was one thing; to find analogies between their prophets of doom, including Jesus, and Roman philosophy was intolerable. If things were bad all over, Cyprian said confidently, it is the God of heaven and earth, the God and father of Jesus Christ, who makes it so. The empire is weakening as Christianity grows strong. Hauled first before the proconsul Paternus, Cyprian was by turns cagey and stubborn, refusing to be an informer on his fellow priests. For his refusal to denounce Christianity and conform to the Roman rites, he was sentenced to exile, then recalled by Galerius Maximus (Paternus' successor as proconsul) for a second round of questioning. Stubborn as before, the old man ran afoul of Galerius' short temper and was sentenced to death by beheading. According to Prudentius, who preserves his story, Cyprian's followers begged "with one voice" to be killed with him.

On 31 March 297, under the emperor Diocletian, the Manichean religion was outlawed. Like Christianity it was an "import" of dubious vintage. More particularly, it was Persian, and Rome was at war with Persia. Holy books and priests were seized and burned without much ado. Professing members of the cult were put to death without trial. The most prominent Roman Manicheans (the so-called *honestiores*) were spared, but their property was confiscated and they were sent to work in the mines. The process against the Manicheans boded worse things to come for the Christians.

Diocletian published his first decree against the Christians in February 303. The church historian Lactantius (ca. 240–320) writes that Diocletian was a victim of his advisers, and especially of his Caesar of the East, Galerius, "who would have had anyone who refused the sacrifices burnt alive." In fact, Diocletian seems to have been something of a ditherer. Lactantius says it was his tragic flaw to take the credit for his successes by claiming he acted on his own, and to blame all failures on his advisers. The persecution of 303 was such a decision. Diocletian's original position was pragmatic and straightforward: There are simply too many Christians throughout the empire. Blood will flow; uprisings will follow. Besides, most of them will go to their deaths eagerly. Why not simply make it illegal for court officials and soldiers to practice the pernicious superstition? Sensing opposition to this commonsense approach, advisers were called in: magistrates, military commanders, and finally—in desperation—a sooth-sayer who had been sent to inquire of the oracle of Apollo at Miletus what the will of the gods might be in this awkward matter. The answer was predictable: Apollo and Galerius were of one mind. The Christians must be stopped. Lactantius notes bemusedly that on the 23rd of February, the feast of Terminus, god of boundaries, the edict to stamp out ("terminate") the Christian religion was issued. It was the nineteenth year of the reign of Diocletian and just around Easter when word was sent out that Christian buildings were to be destroyed, the sacred books burned, heads of households arrested, and the presbyters compelled to sacrifice to the state gods.

In a famous incident at Cirta in May 303, only two months after the edict was issued, the mayor of the city, accompanied by a posse, arrived at the door of the house which the Christians used as a meeting place. Although interested in getting a record of all "readers" (clergy) in the church, the mayor was also instructed to inventory the church plate and holdings, and to confiscate all copies of scripture. The task proved slippery. The cooperation of the bishop's staff varied: some readers produced books without demur; others vacillated; still others refused. If the description of the inquest at Cirta is typical of the search-and -seize procedures required by the edict, the detective work was thorough and unrelenting. The posse moved from house to house, relying on the weaker clergy to name names. They found books hidden away in private houses, where the readers had squirreled them for safekeeping, the house-church itself being thought an unsafe repository for the full collection of gospels and epistles.

Diocletian had hoped to cripple the movement. Termination would have meant extermination. But the survival tactics of the movement made police work difficult. Christians had become sly. The enthusiasm for martyrdom was now paralleled by accomplished doubletalk:

Mayor: "Point out the readers or send for them"
Bishop: "You already know who they are."
Mayor: "Bring out your books."

Subdeacons: "We have thrown out everything that was here [in the church]."

Executions increased, especially after rumors reached Galerius that plots against the throne were being fomented in Christian circles. New edicts were issued with regularity, each a little more severe than the one before. The fourth edict (304) required that all the people of a city must sacrifice and offer libations to the gods "as a body," Christians included. Diocletian abdicated, in declining health, in 305; Galerius, now emperor, and the new Caesar of the East, Maximinus Daia, pressed on energetically until April 311, when Galerius—one week before his death—issued an edict of toleration. In the west, the enforcers (Maximian and Constantius) had lost heart and faith in the policy, taking an occasional swipe at a church but not much else. In the provinces, especially North Africa, persecution tended to be more severe. How severe is open to question. The church historian Eusebius (ca. 260–ca. 339) depicts the faithful of Thebes rushing to martyrdom as the net grew tighter; but in Oxyrhynchus, just down the Nile, Christians brought before a magistrate and ordered to sacrifice could authorize a third party, often a pagan relative, to perform the ritual in their behalf, thereby avoiding the contamination involved in doing it themselves. As late as 311–312, the populations of a number of cities (Tyre, Antioch, Nicomedia, and Lycia Pamphylia) addressed petitions against the Christians to Maximinus Daia, who had an active retraining program in place, designed to reeducate lapsed Christians in their pagan heritage.

But the life was going out of the movement to repress Christianity. The pagan critics had not succeeded in stemming the popularity of the movement, and the "persecuting" emperors (except perhaps Diocletian himself) had miscalculated both the numbers and the determination of the faithful. The movement was Rome's Vietnam, a slow war of attrition which had been fought to stop a multiform enemy. Even at their worst under Diocletian, the persecutions had been selective and, in their intense form, short-lived. And (as has been known since the seventeenth century) the number of martyrs was not great.

One of the successes of Christian apologetics was to convince the persecutors in Brer Rabbit fashion that they enjoyed persecution—that death is what they liked best of all. In dying for Christ Jesus, the crown of heavenly glory was theirs. With rare exceptions, the people in the cities and towns of the empire were not inclined to collaborate in the persecutions; Rome had a longstanding reputation for "live and let live," and the rulers' need to get political mileage from an enemy within was quickly detected. The goal of the fourth edict against the Christians in 304, in fact, had been to compel loyalty to unpopular rulers, and in 308 the greatly detested Maximinus tried the same tactic (Eusebius, *Martyrs of Palestine* 9.1-3): "Idol temples were forced to be rebuilt quickly; and people in groups, men and their wives and babies at the breast [were forced] to offer sacrifices and wine-offerings." The tactic was ineffectual, Eusebius says, because even the enforcers had lost the heart to impose the penalties and to support the machinery required for the "sacrifice factories" Maximinus tried to set up.

Unhappy at this failure, he sponsored a literary attack, circulating forged gospels and memoirs containing the stock slanders against Jesus. These were posted in public gathering-places and schoolteachers were required to assign portions of them to children as lessons (Eusebius, *Martyrs of Palestine* 9.4.2-5.2). To substantiate charges against the moral habits of the Christians, Maximinus then hired agents (*duces*) to round up prostitutes from the marketplace in Damascus. Tortured until they confessed to being Christians, they then signed statements to the effect that the churches routinely practiced ritual prostitution and required members to participate in sexually depraved acts. These statements were also distributed to the towns and cities for public display. Desperate times, desperate men, desperate measures.

By the time Galerius issued his edict of toleration in favor of the Christians on 30 April 311 three waves of attack had failed: the erratic policies of emperors from Nero to Marcus Aurelius; the literary and philosophical attacks, carried on in collusion with imperial sponsors; and the more sustained persecutions of the third century, ending in 311. Paganism was dying. Maximinus' plan for "reeducating" Christians in the religion of their ancestors had failed.

After Constantine's conversion—whatever it may have been—only Julian (332–363), his nephew, remained to pick up the baton for the pagan cause. Julian did his best to reestablish the old order. He reorganized the shrines and temples; outlawed the teaching of Christian doctrine in the schools; retracted the legal and financial privileges which the Christians had been accumulating since the early fourth century; wrote polemical treatises against the Christians himself; and—in a clever political maneuver—permitted exiled bishops to return to their sees to encourage power-struggles and dissension within the church. Naturally, the Christians despised him. The distinguished theologian Gregory of Nazianzus had been Julian's schoolmate in Athens, where both learned a love for the classical writers (but where Julian had been converted to Greek humanism). Cyril of Alexandria wrote a long refutation of Julian's *Adversus Christianos* (*Against the Christians*), parts of which hark back to Porphyry and Hierocles. All in all, this pagan interlude— never really a renaissance—lasted only three years, until Julian's death in June 363. While the dying words attributed to him as a paean to Christianity, "You have conquered, Galilean!" are not Julian's, they might as well have been.

In the middle of the period we have just described stands Porphyry of Tyre, so named (his original name was Malchus) because of his native city's prominence as a manufacturing center for the royal purple dye (*porphyreum*). Born in 232, Porphyry was eighteen when the persecution broke out under the emperor Decius. Twelve years later, his dislike for Christianity was firmly established. Porphyry had heard Origen preach, studied the Hebrew scripture, especially the prophets, and the Christian gospels, and found them lacking in literary quality and philosophical sophistication. He had joined a "school" in Rome (ca. 262) run by the famous neoplatonic teacher, Plotinus, where he remained until about 270. In Sicily, following Plotinus' death, and back again in Rome, Porphyry developed an intense dislike for popular religion—or superstition, as the Roman intellectuals of his circle preferred to call it, regarding Christianity as the most pernicious form of a disease infecting the empire. In a work titled *Pros Anebo* he pointed out the defects in the cults. Then he tackled Christian teaching in a work in fifteen books known later as *Kata Christianōn* (*Against the Christians*). Popular until the rescript of Galerius in 311, the work was immediately targeted for destruction by the imperial church, which in 448 condemned all existing copies to be burned. What we know of the book comes from fragments preserved in the context of refutation by Christian teachers such as Eusebius and Apollinarius. Nevertheless Augustine admired Porphyry; Jerome wrote his great commentary on the Book of Daniel to neutralize the philosopher's scathing insights into the nature of biblical prophecy.

It is a convention to say that Porphyry was the most "learned" of the critics of Christianity. Having said this, we should note that the critics of Christianity were not at their intellectual best when writing polemic. It has sometimes been suggested, for example, that the fragments of Porphyry's work preserved by the teacher Macarius Magnes (4th–5th century) cannot belong to Porphyry because they represent the work of a lesser mind. A first-class mind Porphyry certainly was, but the debate was not a strenuous one. From the standpoint of the neoplatonic school, Christianity was contemptible because it was simple. Hence, simple devices and stereotyped arguments were used against it. The gospels were the work of charlatans, while Jesus himself was a criminal and a failure, even from the Jewish perspective. His followers had betrayed him; their chief, the greatest coward of all, was made prince of his church. As a miracle worker, Jesus was a second-rater. The teaching of the Christians is self-contradictory: they look for the end of the world, but what they really want is control of the empire. To worship Jesus as a god is an insult to any god deserving of the name. The sentiments expressed were devastating because they came from someone who knew the sacred books of the Christians and their doctrine intimately. Moreover, in his attack Porphyry denied the Christian teachers their favorite refuge: allegory. Porphyry dealt with the plain sense of words. Having mastered allegorical interpretation as a student of Longinus, he knew the tricks of the trade. Whether speaking of the prophecies of the Book of Daniel or the apocalyptic teaching of the church, he refused to excuse contradiction as "mystery" or misstatement of fact as paradox. The gospel writers were not Homer. Their Greek was, by and large, that of the marketplace. They lacked skill, not honesty, for if they had been dishonest men they would have tried to disguise Jesus' failures or the deficiencies of his apostles. But, as they stood, they were hardly worthy of the reverence with which Romans in increasing numbers treated them.

In the following pages, I have reproduced the pagan critic's words as recorded in the *Apocriticus* of Macarius Magnes, amounting to well over half of those attributed by Adolf von Harnack to Porphyry. Since the appearance of Harnack's collection, *Gegen die Christen*, in 1916, a number of studies have appeared defending and attacking the German historian's conclusions. The result is that opinion is divided over whether the pagan of Macarius' dialogue is Porphyry, a transcriber of Porphyry (as Porphyry was of Plotinus) or someone else. That debate is likely to go on for some time, as occasionally new sentences and phrases are added to the corpus of Porphyry's lost work. My own position, as will become clear from what follows in the critical notes and Epilogue, is that Harnack was by and large right. Macarius was responding to Porphyry, either secreting the identity of his opponent for strategic reasons or, less likely, having only the fragments at his disposal without knowledge of their source. The style, themes, approaches, and conclusions belong ultimately—which is not to say directly— to the great pagan teacher. That his words have been paraphrased, manipulated and occasionally mangled by his ineloquent opponent is also fairly clear. It is regrettable, from the standpoints of the history of theology and philosophy, that Porphyry did not find an Origen or a Cyril of Alexandria to answer him.

Having said this, however, one senses that some of Porphyry's most damaging language has been preserved, as well as the sense of urgency and the deep-seated hostility and suspicion with which he regarded Christian doctrine. The work was written to reproach the Christians for their lack of patriotism—a theme that surfaces as soon as Macarius begins to cite his opponent. It moves on to afford a "rationalistic" appraisal of key figures, beliefs, biblical episodes, and doctrines. If, as I said, the philosopher appears carping rather than profound, it is because the debate between philosophy and the church had become stereotyped by the late third century. The best arguments belonged to the pagans, but popular religion—which Porphyry disliked intensely—was never guided or corrected by good argument. Perhaps one of the most interesting aspects of the debate between Macarius and the pagan is that the philosopher keeps his feet planted firmly in the mud throughout the match. Macarius tries flights of philosophical fancy, and usually ends up back on the ground.

The reader is invited to follow the critical notes and to consult the bibliography at the end for further reading. I have chosen to make my lengthy remarks in a comprehensive Epilogue rather than at the beginning of this work. There are two reasons for this procedure. First, as a student, I often resisted the introductions in anthologies of philosophical works, Greek plays or Shakespeare. I say this shamefacedly, knowing now how much work goes into the making of an introduction. But the worst of them said too much—about the life and times and friends and sources of the writer or author—and the best too little. To this day I remember more about Milton than about *Paradise Lost.* When I moved from philosophy and literature to biblical studies, I soon discovered the wisdom of the fundamentalist dictum, that a good Bible can shed a lot of light on the commentaries. That sentiment may be usefully invoked in this case. Anyone interested in pursuing the Hellenistic context of Porphyry's lost work in a comprehensive fashion may begin by reading the Epilogue.

Second, I think we owe it to Porphyry and his "interpreter(s)" to permit them to speak to us directly. Having been buried—more or less successfully—since 448, the words should be permitted at last to breathe their own air. The current mood in classical and patristic studies is favorable to such an exercise. The critical notes provide a running commentary, and the final section of the Epilogue a discussion of text and translation followed by a bibliography of ancient and modern authors relevant to this study.

If the Epilogue (somewhat permissively titled "From Babylon to Rome") seems ambitious, it is because I think a comprehensive discussion of the "buildup" to the pagan critique of Christianity is an essential part of viewing the struggle itself. Pagan-Christian controversy was a continuation of the interface between Judaism and its enemies and of the synagogue and the church. Such an approach is more useful, I recognize, for the "average" reader than for the specialist. Nonetheless, the debate between Jerusalem and Athens (the church and pagan culture) does not begin in the first or the third century but in the recesses of biblical history. Its archetype is the relationship between Jerusalem and Babylon, or between the Maccabees and Greek culture, just as its later crudescence would be the debate between church and state in an era of secular values. The Epilogue has thus been designed for those who wish to explore the debate more fully.

Credit but in no wise the blame for this project must be shared with those who have invested time and encouragement in its making. My wife, Carolyn, has been judiciously aggravating about seeing it completed; my daughter, Marthe, would like to have seen it completed a hundred times over. They have been patient and consistently hopeful.

I owe to my former colleagues in the Department of Humanities at California State University, Sacramento, and to the University Research scheme of that institution a note of thanks for providing the time to do most of the research and translation for this study during the autumn and spring terms of 1990–91. To Professors Robert Platzner and Stephen Harris goes a special word of thanks. The work was pursued in a less systematic way during my time as head of the History Department in the University of Papua New Guinea, and has been put happily and belatedly to bed at Westminster College, Oxford, where it has been encouraged by the members of the School of Theology.

A Note on the Text
and the Controversy

The following translation and partial reconstruction of the "objections" in the *Apocriticus* of Macarius Magnes is based on the edition of C. Blondel, *Macarii Magnetis quae supersunt, ex inedito codice edidit* (Klincksieck: Paris, 1876). Extensive use has been made of Harnack's apparatus criticus, selection, and annotations (*Porphyrius "Gegen die Christen": 15 Bücher, Zeugnisse und Referate*, Abhandlung der kön. preuss. Akademie der Wissenschaft. phil.-hist. Klasse I [Berlin, 1916]). Occasional reference has been made to T. W. Crafer, *The Apocriticus of Macarius Magnes: Greek Texts, Series I* (London and New York: Macmillan, 1919), running corrections of which can be found in the critical notes accompanying the translation.

The confidence of Harnack, that the *Apocriticus* undoubtedly *reflects* the philosophy of Porphyry, has been challenged repeatedly, before and since 1916, but most significantly by T. D. Barnes, "Porphyry Against the Christians: Date and the Attribution of Fragments," *JTS*, n.s. 24 (1973): 424-42. In turn, there has been a growing skepticism about Barnes' dating of the material and his pessimism about the work's being Porphyry's, notably the work of Robert Waelkens, "L'Économie, thème, apologetique et principe hermeneutique dans l'apocritique de Macarios Magnes," *Recueil de Travaux d'Histoire et de Philologie* (Louvain, 1974). Anyone interested in pursuing the history of guesswork concerning the attribution of fragments may begin with these.

It is my belief that Harnack's painstaking work has not been superseded and that his informed guesswork was substantially correct: that the pagan voice to be heard in the criticisms of Macarius' pagan is none other than Porphyry. Because this translation is not meant to be a contribution to the ascription debate, however, I have outlined my reasons within the text in the critical notes to the translation.

Neither Harnack nor Crafer was unaware of the checkered history of the text of the *Apocriticus* between the ninth and the sixteenth century, nor of the difficulty of identifying the author of the work, Macarius Magnes. In quoting passages from the book against the Protestants, the Jesuit Turianus claimed in the sixteenth century that the book was written by a certain "Magnetes" around 150—which would place the pagan source well out of range of Porphyry. By the time Blondel and Duchesne in the nineteenth century began their editing labors, the preferred "average" date was somewhere in the fourth century—between 300 and 350—with the place of composition being Magnesia or Edessa. As the Germans could not acccept the primacy of French Catholic scholarship on the point, they offered that the work dated from the fifth century, and that its author was the bishop of Magnesia who, in 403, accused Heraclides of Ephesus of following the errors of Origen at the synod of the Oak.

The theory that the "pagan" philosopher cited in the work is Porphyry has been argued since the sixteenth century, with occasional suggestions that Porphyry's pupil Hierocles or one of three pagan critics remembered by the Christians as the "authors of persecution" was the source. The epithet derived from the belief that their literary attacks had incited Aurelian's successors to renew the battle against the spread of Christian teaching. Uncertainties about the date of the work, the authorship of the *Apocriticus* and the identity of the pagan opponent were compounded by the fact that the manuscript tradition itself was spotty: the *Apocriticus* had disappeared from view in the sixteenth century in the vicinity of Venice and was only "discovered" in Athens in 1867.

In 1911, Adolf von Harnack, the great Berlin church historian, entered the debate. Although his conclusions are now challenged by some modern scholars, he argued convincingly that the pagan opponent in the *Apocriticus* is Porphyry and that the work contained material for an edition of his lost treatise *Against the Christians* (*Texte und Untersuchungen 37*, Leipzig, 1911). Harnack was mistaken, I believe, for reasons stated above, in thinking that Macarius did not know the excerpts to have been Porphyry's; in his view, Macarius knew the extracts from a later (anonymous) writer, since at one point the pagan is actually referred to Porphyry's treatise *On Abstinence.*

Crafer (1919) attempted a number of modifications of Harnack's thesis, arguing that the work reflects the "master mind of Porphyry" but is really the work of the philosopher Hierocles. A great deal was made to hang by Crafer on Hierocles' unfavorable comparison between Apollonius of Tyana (whose miracles and feats were said to be greater) and Jesus; the theme is recorded by the pagan in the *Apocriticus*. But as the comparison is a natural one—Celsus had used it in the second century—there is no reason to suppose that Porphyry would not have referred to the Apollonius story.

A comparison of the sayings of the pagan philosopher with the "circumstantial" evidence of patristic quotations and characterizations of the book make it highly probable that Porphyry is at least the inspiration and, in some cases, the actual critical voice of the pagan philosopher in the *Apocriticus*. From it we can draw an adequate, if approximate, view of the nature and scope of pagan objections to the increasingly successful church of the late third century. In theme, philosophical orientation, style, and literary approach the evidence points to Porphyry more directly than to any lesser light.

List of Abbreviations

ANCL   *Ante-Nicene Christian Library* (Edinburgh, 1892; rpt. American Edition: Grand Rapids, Minn., 1977).

CGS   *Die griechischen christlichen Schriftsteller* (Leipzig 1877)

CSEL   *Corpus scriptorum ecclesiasticorum latinorum* (Vienna 1866–1902)

JRS   *Journal of Roman Studies*

JTS   *Journal of Theological Studies*

NHL   *Nag Hammadi Library in English*, ed. James Robinson, Leiden, 1977.

OECT   *Oxford Early Christian Texts*

PG   *Patrologia cursus completus series graeca* (Paris, 1857-66)

PL   *Patrologia cursus completus series latina* (Paris, 1844-55)

ZNTW   *Zeitschrift für die neutestamentliche Wissenschaft*

Translations of patristic, biblical and classical works unless otherwise noted are my own. Titles of patristic sources are given in English unless they are better known by their Latin or Greek names: thus, Augustine, *City of God*; but Origen, *Contra Celsum*.

Against the Christians

The Extracts
of
Macarius Magnes

1

Miscellaneous Objections

Apocrit. II.7-II.12

[Matt. 10.34]*1
The words of Christ, "I came not to bring peace but a sword.
I came to separate a son from his father," belie the true inten-
tions of the Christians. They seek riches and glory. Far from
being friends of the empire, they are renegades waiting for
their chance to seize control.[2]

---

1. II.7-II.12, marked with asterisks, are based on Macarius' replies to
objections that have not survived in the manuscript. (Ed.)

2. This objection is clear from the thrust of Macarius' insistence that
Christ is speaking of spiritual warfare against the power of sin. Christians
take up their cross rather than a sword. The sword is interpreted as that
which cuts relationships between the old (sinful) way of life and the new
life of faith. The image is given an allegorical twist by the Christian teacher:
"The man divided from his father is the apostle of Christ separated from
the law. . . . The sword is the grace of the Gospel." The philosopher's view
that Christians are bad citizens is typical of anti-Christian polemic: cf.
Tertullian, *Apology* 11; *To the Nations* 7. The opinion that the Christians
were politically ambitious was well-established by the fourth century. Justin
writes in his *First Apology* (ca. 168): "If we looked for a human kingdom
we should also deny our Christ that we might not be slain; and we should
strive to escape detection, that we might obtain what we expect. But since
our thoughts are not fixed on the present, we are not concerned when men

[Matt. 12.48-49]*
That Christ is a mere man is proved from the fact that he claimed kinship with his disciples while rejecting ties to his natural family. It is clear that Christ preferred the company of his followers to that of his mother and brothers.[3]

[Mark 10.18]*
That Christ is merely human is proved further from his own mouth, when he rebukes a man in the following terms: "Why do you call me good [when] no one is good except God?"[4]

[Matt. 17.15]*
Christ on occasion shows no more insight than the Jews, for he agrees to cure a boy thought by his father to be a lunatic when in fact it was a demon that was troubling the boy.[5]

---

cut us off, since death also is a debt which must at all events be paid" (*I Apology* 40).

3. It is plausible that Porphyry throughout this section of his attack was challenging the doctrine of the divinity of Jesus (see objection following). The criticism is reminiscent of Celsus' carping treatment of Jesus' ties to his disciples and their final betrayal of his confidence. See my reconstruction in *Celsus On the True Doctrine* (New York: Oxford University Press, 1987), pp. 59, 62-66. Macarius' response to this treatment of Matt. 12.48-49 is a compilation of paraphrased sayings, with this puzzling formulation given to Jesus: "He that believes that I am the only begotten son of God in some sense begets me, not in subsistence but in faith" (*ouk en hypostasei ousias genomenos*).

4. The philosopher misses the irony of Jesus' reply to the rich young man in Mark's gospel. Macarius takes the opportunity to instruct him by paraphrasing Jesus' rebuke as follows: "Why call me good if you think of me only as a man? You are mistaken in addressing me as good if you think of me as a mortal young man, because only in God—not among mortals—does good reside." The remainder of Macarius' response is a tedious discourse on the standard neo-Platonic distinction between relative good (*agathos*) and inherent or absolute good (*arete*).

5. Both the pagan criticism and the Christian account are based on the mistaken idea that Matthew's text is discrete from Mark's account of the episode. In Mark's gospel the father diagnoses the cause of the disease as a dumb spirit of such strength that the disciples cannot cast it out. Matthew's much briefer rendition omits any initial reference to a demon;

[John 5.31]*
Christ contradicts himself and proves himself a liar when he says, "If I bear witness to myself, then my witness is not true." But in saying [John 8.12-13], "I am the light of the world" (and other, similar things) he does bear witness to himself—just as he is accused of doing.[6]

---

thus Macarius' reply: "The serpent was crafty enough to wage its campaign against the little boy during the changes in the moon, such that everyone would think that his affliction was caused by its influence."

6. Macarius takes Jesus to mean that if he were a man then bearing witness to himself would be untrue. Instead, he seeks attestation from God, as God; thus there is divine attestation for Jesus' claim to be the light of the world.

2

Critique of the Gospels and Their Authors

Apocrit. II.12–II.15

The evangelists were fiction writers—not observers or eye-witnesses to the life of Jesus. Each of the four contradicts the other in writing his account of the events of his suffering and crucifixion.

One [writer] records that on the cross someone filled a sponge with vinegar and thrust it at him [Mark 15.36]. Another [Matt. 27.33] denies this, saying, "When they had come to the place called The Skull, they gave him wine and gall mixed to drink, but when he had tasted it he would not drink."

Further he says, "About the ninth hour Jesus cried with a loud voice saying, *Eloi, Eloi—lama sabacthani,* which is, 'My God, my God why have you forsaken me?' "

Another [John 19.29] writes, "There was a pot filled with vinegar [which they] strapped [to a rod?] with reeds and held it to his mouth. And after he had taken the vinegar [Jesus] cried out with a loud voice and said, 'It is over'; and bowing his head he gave up his spirit."

But [Luke] says "He cried out with a loud voice and said 'Father into your hands I will deliver [*parathēsomai*] my spirit' " (Luke 23.46).

Based on these contradictory and secondhand reports, one might think this describes not the suffering of a single individual but of several! Where one says "Into your hands I *will* deliver my spirit," another says "It *is* finished" and another "My God, my God, why have you forsaken me," and another "My God, my God why do you punish me?"

It is clear that these addled legends are lifted from accounts of several crucifixions or based on the words of someone who died twice [*dis thanatounta* for *dusthanatounta,* i.e., dying a difficult death: Crafer] and did not leave a strong impression of his suffering and death to those present. [It follows that] if these men were unable to be consistent with respect to the way he died, basing [their account] simply on hearsay, then they did not fare any better with the rest of their story.[7]

[John 19.33-35]
From other sources it can be shown that the story of [the death of Jesus] was a matter of guesswork.

"And when they came to Jesus, seeing that he was already dead, they did not break his legs. But one of the soldiers pierced his side with a lance, and immediately there came blood and water."

Only John says this—none of the others. No wonder John

---

7. Rather puzzlingly Macarius designates the philosopher's view "Hellenic" and then employs allegory to override the literatim contradictions in the texts cited; thus, what appear to be inconsistencies are taken to be peculiarities of style: "the truth is not to be sought by looking for facts in syllables and letters." Macarius soon tires of this defense, however, and takes up the claim that the eyewitnesses were drunk with fear, owing to "the earthquake and the crash of rocks around them" (cf. Matt. 27.51-53). Their eagerness to preserve a record of the things happening around them resulted in a fractured and haphazard style, which Macarius excuses as proof of their zeal to preserve the truth. Interesting as well is Macarius' comparison of the evangelists' accounts to the writing of Herodotus: the gospels are more to be trusted because their authors lacked education and did not "adorn their writings with clever rhetorical devices." Perhaps the most remarkable feature of Macarius' defense is his praise for the subtlety of Greek education and his castigation of the Romans as *barbaros ethnos,* "barbarians like the Jews."

is so anxious to swear to the truthfulness of his account, saying, "He that saw it testifies to it—and we know his testimony is true."

This looks to me like the statement of a simpleton. How can a statement be true when it refers to nothing? A man can [only] witness to something that really happened, not to something fashioned from thin air.[8]

There is another way to refute the false opinion concerning the resurrection of [Jesus], which is spoken of everywhere these days. Why did this Jesus (after his crucifixion and rising—as your story goes) not appear to Pilate, who had punished him saying he had done nothing worthy of execution, or to the king of the Jews, Herod, or to the high priest of the Jewish people, or to many men at the same time, as for example to people of renown among the Romans, both senators and others, whose testimony was reliable.[9]

Instead he appeared to Mary Magdalene, a prostitute who came from some horrible little village and had been possessed by seven demons, and another Mary, equally unknown, probably a peasant woman, and others who were of no account.

---

8. Macarius does not deal with the substance of the philosopher's argument, viz., that uncorroborated statements have less force than multiple testimony. Porphyry takes the silence of the three synoptic writers as evidence that the events described in John 19.33f. did not happen and finds the writer's introduction of self-referring testimony simplistic. It is possible that the philosopher had also referred to the absence of the apostles from the other accounts of the crucifixion (cf. Mark 14.50; 15.40). If so, Macarius does not take up the point. His stratagem is to treat John's account allegorically; thus, "Blood and water flowed like a stream so that those [Jews] who dwelled in a land of bondage might be delivered by the blood and those [gentiles] who had the stripes of their sins could be washed in water."

9. Celsus makes the same point in the *Alēthēs logos*: "Who really saw [his rising from the dead]? A hysterical woman, as you admit, and perhaps one other person—both deluded by his sorcery, or perhaps so wrenched with grief at his failure that they hallucinated him risen from the dead by a sort of wishful thinking. . . . If this Jesus were trying to convince anyone of his powers then surely he ought to have appeared first to the Jews who treated him so badly, and to his accusers—indeed, to everyone, everywhere" (Hoffmann, *Celsus*, pp. 65, 67).

Still, he promised, "You will see the son of man sitting on the right hand of power and coming on clouds." [Matt. 24.30] Had he shown himself to people who could be believed, then others would have believed through them—and [Christians] would not today be punished for fabricating these ridiculous tales.

It cannot be pleasing to God that so many should suffer horrible punishment on his account.[10]

[John 12.31]

Anyone will recognize that the [gospels] are really fairy tales if he takes time to read further into this nonsense of a story, where Christ says, "Now has come the judgment of the world; now shall the world ruler be cast out."

Tell me, for heaven's sake, what sort of judgment is this supposed to be—and just who is the "ruler" who is being cast outside? If you answer, "The emperor [is the ruler]," I say that there is no single world ruler—as many have power in the world—and none have been "cast down." If, on the other hand, you mean someone who is not flesh and blood but an immortal, then where would he be thrown? Where is this invisible world ruler to go outside the world he rules?

Show us from your record. If there isn't another world for this ruler to go to—and it is impossible for there to be two such worlds—then where other than to the world he's to be expelled from *can* he go?

One cannot be cast out of what he is already in. Unless of course you are thinking in terms of a clay pot which, when broken, spills its contents not into oblivion but into the air or the earth, or the like.

---

10. The logic of the philosopher's argument is that an event like the resurrection of Jesus, while not in itself impossible, demands credible witnesses—"men of high renown"—whereas the Christian record in the gospels introduces witnesses whose reports are dubious, coming as they do from the lowest strata of society.

Macarius replies by saying that the resurrection was not made known to Pilate or to the Jews in order to prevent the fact from being covered up. Instead, "he appeared in the flesh to women who were unable to persuade anyone of his rising."

Perhaps you mean that when the world is broken (but this is impossible!) the one inside it will then be outside of it like a nut out of its shell. But what exactly is this outside like? What are its length, breadth, depth, features?

Of course, if it has these things then it, too, is a world. And for what reason would a ruler of the world be expelled from a world to which he is no stranger. For if he were a stranger to the world, he could not have ruled it: and who [would be equipped] to force the ruler out of this world against his will?

Or do you mean he goes willingly? Clearly you imagine he will be cast out against his will: that is plain from the record. To be "cast out" is to be expelled against one's own choice. But normally the wrong attaches to the man who uses force, not to the one who resists it.

This silliness in the gospels ought to be taught to old women and not to reasonable people. Anyone who should take the trouble to examine these facts more closely would find thousands of similar tales, none with an ounce of sense to them.[11]

---

11. A number of points raised by Porphyry resemble the criticisms of Celsus and Marcion's critique of orthodox doctrine. Both regarded the world ruler as the lawful proprietor of the world (Hoffmann, *Celsus*, pp. 90-92; Tertullian, *Against Marcion* 3.3.4).

His castigation by an alien god—the *agnostos theos* of Marcionite speculation—is seen as an act of usurpation. Any world into which he might be cast would amount to exile—punishment usually reserved for pretenders rather than for rightful rulers. Crafer (p. 46) observes that Porphyry's reference to the multitude of rulers who have not been deposed by the new world ruler (Christ?) comes from a time following Diocletian's subdivision of the Empire in C.E. 292. The political ambitions of the Christians seem to have been a favorite target for philosophical ridicule of this kind: cf. II.vii. The theme of proprietorship can also be observed in gnostic sources; cf. the Nag Hammadi treatise, "On the Origin of the World," NHL II.97, in Robinson, pp. 162-63.

3

The Ruler and End of the World

Apocrit. II.16

[John 7.43–4]

Let us review that dark saying which Jesus directed at the Jews when he said, "You do not receive my word because your father is that devil the Slanderer, and you do the whims of your father."

Tell us, who exactly is this Slanderer who is the father of the Jews? For in the normal course of things anyone who does what his father tells him is acting correctly in obeying a parent, out of respect for the parent. If a father is wicked, then the sins of the father must not be attributed to his children. So who is this father who prevented [the Jews] from listening to Christ?

When the Jews said, "We have [but] one father and that is God," Jesus retorted, "[No], you are of your father the Slanderer." So I ask, Who and where is this Slanderer? From what act of slander does he get his name? "Slanderer" cannot be his birth-name, but a name that comes from something he did. Among what race of people did he appear and commit his act of slander? [Normally] it is those who accept the slander who appear guilty of an offense; those who are slandered are merely the victims. And it could be argued that it is not the Slanderer who did wrong but the one who gave him an excuse for slander.

If a man puts an obstacle in the road [with the intention of blocking someone's way], and someone comes along and trips over it in the dark, it is the man who put it there who is responsible for the fall—not the man who stumbles. So, too, the man who causes slander is guilty of a greater wrong than those who use it or those who are hurt by it.

Is this Slanderer a man of passion? If he is not he would never have slandered—but if he is subject to human weaknesses, then he ought to be forgiven what he has done, just as we forgive those who are sick and frail and do not hold them responsible for their ailments.[12]

---

12. Porphyry's suggestion is that an evil father capable of enforcing obedience is the source of evil. His agents or children have no choice but to obey and in so doing at least uphold the virtue of filial respect and loyalty. The equivalent point is made in a different context by the heretic Marcion, who maintained that the "just" God of the Old Testament is the ultimate source of human failings, as his laws and demands are incoherent and contradictory (Tertullian, *Against Marcion* 1.16.5). The philosopher may have had some such critique in mind. The disjunctive proposition that follows dictates Macarius' response: either the slanderer is moved by human affections or he is not. If he is not, then he would not have slandered. If he is, then he must be forgiven for his failings as the Christian God forgives others. To win his point, Macarius makes the best of ambiguities in the translation of the verse, arguing that *humeis ek tou patros tou diabolou este* (John 8.44) means "You are of the father of the Slanderer," rather than "You are of your father, the slanderer." But the point is oblique.

4

The Life and Work of Jesus

Apocrit. III.1–III.6

When brought before the high priest and Roman governor, why didn't Jesus say anything to suggest he was wise or divine?[13] He could have taught his judge and his accusers how to become better men! But, no: he only manages to be whipped and spit on and crowned with briars—unlike Apollonius who talked back to the emperor Domitian, vanished from the palace and soon was to be seen by many in the city of Dicearchia, now called Puteoli.[14]

---

13. Crafer notes that the questions posed by Porphyry are simpler and more direct than Macarius' turgid and diffuse responses would indicate (p. 51, n. 2). While Macarius says that the philosopher sought to win the debate through the loftiness of his Attic oratory, it seems clear from the diction in III.1 that Macarius often undertakes to summarize his opponent's most salient objections with his own response in view. Some turns in the response are dictated by nuances that have not been preserved in Macarius' representation of the objections.

14. Apollonius of Tyana, a neo-Pythagorean philosopher who died ca. 90, was a favorite subject for anti-Christian writers from the second century. The biography of Apollonius written by Philostratus around 220 was composed deliberately to emphasize its similarities with the gospels. Hierocles, a pupil of Porphyry, used it in 303 (the year of Porphyry's death) to write his own life of Apollonius, designed to deny the uniqueness of Christian doctrine.

And even if Christ's suffering was carried out according to God's plan, even if he was meant to suffer punishment—at least he might have faced his suffering nobly and spoken words of power and wisdom to Pilate, his judge, instead of being made fun of like a peasant boy in the big city.[15]

[Matt. 26.36ff.]
There is, in addition, a saying [of Jesus] which is both stupid and unclear, that which he spoke to his disciples when he said, "Do not fear those who can kill the body."

When [Jesus] himself agonizes in expectation of his death, he prays that his suffering might be eliminated; and he says to his friends, "Wait, pray, so that temptation may not overcome you." Surely such sayings are not worthy of a son of God, nor even of a wise man who hates death.[16]

---

15. Porphyry voices what had become a stock objection to the divinity of Jesus, namely that divinity is susceptive of proof and that at the point where such proof might have been expected Jesus produces none. This in turn is contrasted with the legend of Apollonius of Tyana. Both Nero and Domitian condemned his teaching as seditious, but he escaped punishment by miraculous means in each case. Porphyry regards such escapes as heroic, as did Celsus (Hoffmann, *Celsus*, pp. 70–72). Jesus' failure to duplicate such feats is cited as evidence against Christian belief in his divinity. Celsus had made the additional point that if apotheosis is the hallmark of divinity, then only figures such as Asklepios, Herakles, and Dionysus are worthy of reverence, owing to the greater antiquity of their stories. Macarius argues that Jesus' conduct during his trial and passion was in strict conformity with prophecy.

16. The reply to this objection seems especially muddled. Macarius argues that Jesus only pretends to be afraid of death, as a ruse to bring about the passion more quickly—in short, as a means of teasing Satan into thinking that he is vulnerable to temptation "as a man might stir up a wild beast by making a noise." Macarius continues: "So, he really wants the cup to come quickly, not to pass away. And observe that he calls it a cup, not suffering, for a cup represents good cheer." The logic here envisaged can be explored more fully in the the arguments of the church fathers who supposed that Christ bared his humanity as "bait" in order to catch Satan on the hook of his divinity. See, e.g, Justin Martyr, *Dialogue with the Jew Trypho* 72; Irenaeus, *Against Heresies* 4.33. However ingenious Macarius' defense, however, it seems to have little to do with Porphyry's objection.

[John 5.46-7]
"If you believed Moses, then you would believe me. For he wrote about me." The saying is filled with stupidity! Even if [Moses] said it, nothing of what he wrote has been preserved; his writings are reported to have been destroyed along with the Temple. All the things attributed to Moses were really written eleven hundred years later by Ezra and his contemporaries.

And even if [the Law] could be considered as the work of Moses, it does not prove that Christ was a god, or the word of God, or of the creator. Further: who [among the Jews] has ever spoken of a crucified Christ?[17]

[Matt. 8.31; Mark 5.1]
If we turn our attention to [the Christian] account, it can be shown to be pure deceit and trickery. Matthew writes that Christ met up with two demon[iacs] who lived among the tombs and that, being afraid, they entered into swine, many of which were killed.

Mark exaggerates when he says there was a great number of swine; "Jesus said to him, Go out of him you unclean spirit, from this man. And he asked him, What is your name, and he answered, *Many*. And he begged him [Jesus] that he should not be expelled from the country. And a herd of swine was feeding. And the demons begged that they might be permitted to enter into the swine. And when they had entered into the

---

The bifurcation of the humanity and divinity of Jesus was rejected at the Council of Chalcedon in 451. Porphyry's more general point seems to be that Jesus did not accept death as a true philosopher would have done.

17. The philosopher shows a surprising awareness of the history of the biblical text in denying the traditional attribution of the the books of the law to Moses. Macarius acknowledges the implications of the biblical account (Neh. 13.1-3), but suggests that the Holy Spirit had dictated the law to Moses and to Ezra alike. A feature of the philosopher's argument, not here represented by Macarius but evident in his reply, is the notion that Ezra copied portions of the law incorrectly. In Porphyry's *Philosophy from Oracles* it is stated that the followers of Jesus misunderstood and misrepresented his teaching in the gospels.

swine, they rushed down the steep into the sea—about two thousand—and were choked; and they that fed them fled" [Mark 5.8ff.]

What a story! What nonsense! What an offense to reason! Two thousand swine splashing into the sea, choking and dying![18]

It is rumored as well that the demons begged Jesus not to throw them over the cliff's edge and that he agreed to their request, sending them instead into the swine: and does not one react to this fable by saying, "What complete foolishness— what deceit—that Jesus should conspire to grant the wishes of evil spirits who were stalking the world to carry out their murderous designs!"

What the demons were asking was to dance through the land of the living and to make the world their toy. They would have stirred the sea till it overflowed its boundaries and filled the world with sorrow. They would have awakened the powers of the earth and unleashed their anger on the world until chaos was restored. Tell me: was it fair that Jesus softened his heart for these monsters who wished to do only evil—that he should have sent them where they wanted to go instead of into the abyss—where they deserved to go?

If the story is true and not a fable (as we hold it to be), what does it say about Christ, that he permitted the demons to continue to do harm by driving them out of one man and into some poor pigs? [Not only this], but he causes the swineherds to run for their lives and sends a whole city into a panic.

Odd that someone who alleges to have come into the world to patch up the harm [done by the evil one] to all mankind should limit himself to helping out just one. To free only one man from the spiritual bondage [of sin] and not two, or three, or thirteen, or everyone—or to free certain people of their fears

---

18. At least the initial part of the critique is an interesting example of pagan synoptic criticism. It is Matthew who is probably guilty of the greater exaggeration, turning Mark's single demoniac into two possessed men. Matthew specifies a "large number" of swine, where Mark gives "about two thousand"—a little less than half the number required to accommodate a legion of demons.

while making others afraid—this seems to me the opposite of morality. It looks to me like treachery!

Furthermore, in permitting enemies to do what they like by moving to another abode, [Jesus] acts like a king who ruins his own kingdom. After all, if a king is unable to drive the barbarians out of every country he will usually drive them from one place to another, pushing back the evil from one place to the next.

Does Christ in the same way—being unable to drive the demons from his territory—send them as far as he *can* send them, namely into the unclean beasts? If so, he does indeed do something marvelous and worth talking about. But it is also the sort of action that raises questions about his [divine] powers.

A reasonable person, upon hearing such a tale, instinctively makes up his mind as to the truthfulness of the story; he says something like, "If Christ does not do his good for the benefit of everything under the sun, but only relocates the evil by driving it from place to place, and if he takes care of some and neglects others—well, then, what good is he as a savior?"

By this sort of action, he who *is* saved only makes life impossible for someone else who is not, so that the unsaved stand to accuse those who are saved.[19] In my judgment, it is best to regard such a story as fiction. If you regard the story as anything other than fiction then there is plenty even for a fool to laugh at.[20]

---

19. Porphyry's point seems somewhat blunted by Macarius' response. The thrust of the objection to Matthew's account of the demoniac is that it contradicts Christian belief in Jesus as savior of the whole world: the limits and purpose of his actions are revealed in his inability or unwillingness to defeat the powers of evil in an unambiguous way. Instead, he "relocates" evil (thus the swine, the Jews, or the ones who reject the gospel) and creates a class of victims who do not participate in the salvation he is supposed to offer. That great numbers do not participate in these blessings proves to the philosopher that Jesus did not intend to save everyone—in which case his goodness is questionable, or else he was unable to do so, which argues against his divinity.

20. Note Eusebius' description of the style of Porphyry's work against the Christians: "Porphyry, who settled in our day in Sicily, issued treatises against us, attempting in them to slander the sacred scriptures" (*Ecclesiastical History* 6.19.2f.).

Can anyone tell me what business a large herd of swine had roaming about the hills of Judah, given that the Jews had always regarded them as the vilest and most detested form of animal life? And how is it that those swine choked as they are supposed to have done, when they were cast—not into the *ocean*—into a mere *lake*? I leave it to infants to decide the truthfulness of such a tale![21]

[Matt. 19.24]

I turn now to test another saying, one even more confusing than the last, as when Jesus says, "It is easier for a camel to go through a needle [*sic*] than for a rich man to enter the kingdom of heaven.

If it is true that a rich man who has kept himself free from the sins of the flesh—murder, thievery, adultery, cheating and lying, fornication, blasphemy—is prohibited from getting any sort of heavenly reward, what use is it for rich men to be good? [And if the poor are the only ones destined for heaven] what's the harm in in their committing any offense they like?

---

21. Macarius replies mistakenly that Matthew mentions two *demons* "but does not say that two men were possessed by them" (cf. Matt. 8.28), thus duplicating Porphyry's misreading. Macarius here and elsewhere shows a tendency to view the story as support for incipient Christological views of the fourth century. Thus he imagines that the demons were scorched by the searching rays of Christ's divine nature and craved the soothing waters for relief of their torture, using the swine "as a kind of ladder, since they themselves were of an incorporeal nature." As to the criticism that the Jews would have had no business keeping animals forbidden to them under Mosaic law, Macarius responds correctly that the scene is not laid in a Jewish but a Roman *sedeo* or gentile settlement. Although Mark does not make the location clear, the Greek *peran* would normally mean the east side of the lake. Some versions read Gerasa (modern Jerash), a Syro-Greek city of the Decapolis league. Other versions have Gadara, which is evidently what Matthew accepted (Matt. 8.28). The Sinaitic Syriac, Bohairic, Armenian and Ethiopic versions of Mark 5.1 read "Gergesenes," Gergesa being hypothetically located on the immediate eastern boundary of the lake at el-Kursi. In any event, it was a part of the pre-Marcan tradition to see Jesus' crossing of the lake as a celebration of the taking of the gospel to non-Jews, and the demoniac himself was understood to be a gentile.

For it seems it is not virtue that gets a man into heaven but poverty.

Just as wealth appears to keep a rich man out of heaven, being poor gets a pauper in! And so it's the rule that a poor man can ignore virtue; and what is more, he can trust that his poverty alone will save him no matter what kind of evil things he does. Meantime the rich are closed out of the heavenly sanctuary, since

"Poverty saves."

It seems unlikely to me that these words belong to Christ. They ring untrue to the ear. They seem to be rather the words of poor people who wish to deprive the rich of their property. Why, only yesterday [Christian teachers] succeeded—through quoting the words, "Sell what you have and give it to the poor and you shall have treasure in heaven"—in depriving noble women of their savings.[22]

They were persuaded to squander what they had on the beggars, giving away what was rightly theirs and making themselves beggars in return. They were turned from having to wanting, from rich to poor, from freedom to slavery and from being wealthy to being pitiful! In the end, [these same women] were reduced to going from door to door to the houses of the well-off to beg—which is the nethermost point of disgrace and humiliation.

They lost what belonged to them in the name of "godliness" and they learned, as a result, what it is to crave the goods of other people. The words [here ascribed to Jesus] look rather to be the words of some woman in distress![23]

---

22. A useful point of reference for this accusation is Tertullian's *Apology* 39, where the common life of the Christian church as a charitable organization is described. The view that women are duped by Christian "beggars" is conventional in anti-Christian polemic. Celsus (Origen, *Contra Celsum* 1.9) had compared Christian teachers to the begging priests of Cybele.

23. Porphyry's criticism of the poverty ethic of the gospel is far-reaching and anticipates some of the form-critical evaluations of the sayings of Jesus advanced much later in the history of the synoptic gospels. With Celsus (cf. *Contra Celsum* 3.44), Porphyry regards certain sayings of Jesus to reflect attitudes arising out of the small and generally impoverished Christian com-

[Matt. 14.25; Mark 6.48]

Another section in the gospel deserves comment, for it is likewise devoid of sense and full of implausibility; I mean that absurd story about Jesus sending his apostles across the sea ahead of him after a banquet, then walking across to them "at the fourth watch of the night." It is related that they had been working all night to keep the boat adrift and were frightened by the size of the storm [surging against the boat]. (The fourth watch would be the tenth hour of the night, with three hours being left.)

Those who know the region well tell us that, in fact, there is no "sea" in the locality but only a tiny lake which springs from a river that flows through the hills of Galilee near Tiberias. Small boats can get across it within two hours. [And the lake is too small] to have seen whitecaps caused by storm. Mark seems to be stretching a point to its extremities when he writes that Jesus—after nine hours had passed—decided in the tenth to walk across to his disciples who had been floating about on the pond for the duration!

As if this isn't enough, he calls it a "sea"—indeed, a stormy sea—a very angry sea which tosses them about in its waves causing them to fear for their lives. He does this, apparently, so that he can next show Christ miraculously causing the storm to cease and the sea to calm down, hence saving the disciples from the dangers of the swell. It is from fables like this one

---

munities of the empire. He finds it ludicrous that such attitudes should serve as criteria for heavenly rewards, or that Jesus should have made wealth an obstacle to salvation. However, the criticism is socially rather than philosophically framed. The Platonism of many Christian writers of the fourth century tended to support such an interpretation of the gospels, especially such passages as Matt. 19.24, Mark 10.17ff. and Luke 12.13ff., which emphasized the implicit anti-materialism of Jesus' condemnation of wealth. Macarius' response should be viewed against the tendency to interpret the socially conditioned poverty ethic of the gospels in an idealistic or Platonic fashion: "The burden of wealth shows itself as a disease in mankind . . . and it is by far better to shed the burden and ascend unencumbered to the heavenly ranks above." Cf. Plotinus, 4 *Ennead* 8.1-8; Augustine, *City of God* 13.16.

that we judge the gospel to be a cleverly woven curtain, each thread of which requires careful scrutiny.[24]

---

24. Apart from quibbles over nomenclature (Macarius argues that any gathering of water can go by the generic name "sea," as Mark had located the boat *en mesō tēs thalassēs*), the rebuttal centers on the spiritual meaning of the episode. Against Porphyry's commonsense approach to the text, Macarius argues that the story illustrates the two natures of Christ, who first terrifies his disciples through his godhead in creating the storm, then pities them in his manhood, and finally shows his dominion over nature by causing the storm to abate: "The sea denotes the brine and gall of human existence; the night is life; the boat is the world; those who sail at night are human beings; the hostile wind is the power of the devil; and the fourth watch is the coming of the savior."

5

The Sayings of Jesus

Apocrit. III.7–III.18

[Matt. 26.11; Matt. 28.20]
In a short saying attributed to him, Christ says to his disciples,
"You will always have the poor among you, but me you will
not always have." The occasion for the sermon is this: A certain
woman takes an alabaster container filled with ointment and
pours it over Jesus' head. When [his disciples] complain about
the inappropriateness of the action Jesus replies, "Why trouble
the woman when she has done something good for me."

The disciples caused quite a stir, wondering why the ointment, expensive as it was, had not been sold at a profit and
distributed to the poor to ease their hunger. Thus Jesus' non-
sensical response: Poor people there will always be; but he
will not always be with them. [Odd, therefore], that elsewhere
he can say with such confidence, "I shall be with you until
the end of the world."[25]

---

25. Macarius is concerned in his reply to distinguish between the two
"modes" of Christ's discourse, each corresponding to one of the natures: thus
his words to the disciples on the occasion of the woman's extravagance
(Matt. 26.11) underscore the reality of the human nature and point toward
the passion, "but after the passion, having overcome death [Matt. 28.20],
man had become God . . . whose power is not limited by time or space,
but is present always and everywhere."

48

[John 6.54][26]
A famous saying of the Teacher is this one: "Unless you eat my flesh and drink my blood, you will have no life in yourselves." This saying is not only beastly and absurd; it is more absurd than absurdity itself and more beastly than any beast: that a man should savor human flesh or drink the blood of a member of his own family or people—and that by doing this he should obtain eternal life!

Tell us: in recommending this sort of practice, do you not reduce human existence to savagery of a most unimaginable sort? Rumor herself has not heard of such a weird twist on the practice of impiety. The shades of the Furies had not made such practices known even to barbarians. Even the Potideans[27] would not have stooped to such a thing had they not been starving. Thyestes' banquet became [a feast of flesh] due to a sister's grief, and Tereus the Thracian ate such food against his will. Again: Harpagus was tricked by Astyages into eating the flesh of his beloved—also against his will. Yet no one of sound mind has ever made such a dinner!

No one learned this sort of foulness from a chef. True, if you look up Scythian [practices] in the history books, or delve into the habits of the Macrobian Ethiopians, or if you venture out to sea to lands dotted through the world, you will certainly find people who feed on roots or eat reptiles or mice— but they stop short of eating human flesh.

And so, what does this saying mean? Even if it carries

26. In keeping with the dialogue format, Macarius introduces a paragraph contrived to suggest a fresh attack of the Greek upon the Christian. The incipient words in this section are doubtless those of Macarius himself.

27. The Potideans were citizens of a Corinthian colony founded ca. 600 B.C.E. for trade with Macedonia. The colonists defended their port against a number of sieges, notably one by Artabazus (480–479 B.C.E.), resorting to eating their dead as a means of survival. Porphyry's point is that cannibalism has been practiced only in time of necessity or through deceit. The Christians, however, seem to boast about their love feasts. The charge is a recapitulation of the familiar accusation against Christians; cf. the *Octavius* of Minucius Felix, trans. G. H. Rendell (Cambridge, Mass: Harvard University Press, 1931).

some hidden meaning, that does not excuse its appearance, which seems to suggest that men are less than animals. No tale designed to fool the simple-minded is crueler or more deceptive [than this myth of the Christians].[28]

[Mark 16.18]
In another passage Jesus says: "These signs shall witness to those who believe: they shall lay hands on the sick and they shall recover. And if they drink any deadly drug, it will hurt them in no way." Well then: the proper thing to do would be to use this process as a test for those aspiring to be priests, bishops or church officers. A deadly drug should be put in front of them and [only] those who survive drinking it should be elevated in the ranks [of the church].

If there are those who refuse to submit to such a test, they may as well admit that they do not believe in the things that Jesus said. For if it is a doctrine of [Christian] faith that men can survive being poisoned or heal the sick at will, then the believer who does not do such things either does not believe them, or else believes them so feebly that he may as well not believe them.[29]

---

28. Scathing as is this criticism of Jesus' saying and Christian eucharistic practice, the pagan polemic had become stereotyped by Macarius' day and seems to be introduced here out of convenience rather than for its timeliness. Macarius has little trouble demolishing the literalism of his opponent's critique, in the process of advancing his own theory of the mystical presence of Christ in the eucharistic bread. For parallels to the philosopher's critique of early Christian eucharistic teaching, see especially the description offered by Marcus Cornelius Fronto (ca. 150), quoted by Minucius Felix, *Octavius* 9.5.6. Porphyry is evidently aware that the Christians interpret the eucharistic words of Jesus allegorically. His real complaint seems to be that the uneducated would not understand the words in their spiritual or mystical sense.

29. As elsewhere, the philosopher bases his objection on the literal meaning of the text. In doing so he is almost certainly working at some historical distance from his Christian opponent, whose response shows no sympathy for the faith-healing practices of the early church. Isolated sects such as the Ophites or Naasenes mentioned by Hippolytus (*Refutation* 5.7.1; cf. Irenaeus, *Against Heresies* 1.30), continued to attribute special significance to the serpent as a symbol of gnosis. And in gnostic exegesis (cf. *Apocryphon*

[Matt. 17.20]
A saying similar to this runs as follows: "Even if you have
faith no bigger than a mustard seed, I tell you in truth that
if you say to this mountain, Be moved into the sea—even that
will be possible for you." It seems to follow that anyone who
is unable to move a mountain by following these directions
is unworthy to be counted among the faithful. So there you
are: not only the ordinary Christians, but even bishops and
priests, find themselves excluded on the basis of such a saying.[30]

---

of John 2.1.22, in Robinson, p. 111), the serpent tempts Adam to be disobedient
to the world ruler. In the cult of Asklepios the snake symbolized the healing
power of the god (cf. Aristophanes, *Plut.* 653-747), though there is no evidence
that the Asclepiadae (the ancient cult of priest-physicians) used snake-
handling as such in their ritual healings. The medicinal or healing value
of the eucharist was a feature of some marginal Christian communities,
notably the Marcosians mentioned by Irenaeus late in the second century,
who used potions and philters, as well as sleight of hand, in their eucharistic
rituals (*Against Heresies* 1.13). In the early second century, Ignatius of
Antioch referred to the eucharist as the *pharmakon tēs zoēs*—the "medicine
of immortality"—perhaps voicing a popular perception of the time as to the
sacrament's healing properties (*To the Ephesians* 20.2).

The philosopher seems to be in touch with a transitional phase in the
teaching of the church, when faith-healing and magical arts, as accoutrements
of the eucharistic celebration, were being eliminated. Hence, Macarius warns
that Mark 16.18 should not be taken literally, since sometimes even
unbelievers recover from deadly drugs. More problematical is Macarius'
suggestion that one cannot take the saying concerning laying hands on the
sick literally.

30. Macarius' response to this criticism is sensitive to the context of
Matt. 17.19-20, which seems to locate Jesus immediately following the
Transfiguration at the foot of a mountain. Following the failure of the disciples
to cure an epileptic child, Jesus is said to compare the resilience of the demon
to an immovable object. Satisfied that the philosopher had misread the
hyperbole, Macarius remarks sarcastically that Jesus himself is not known
to have moved mountains, and that a believer would in any case be prevented
from doing so by the words of Ps. 92.1 ("He made the world which shall
not be shaken"). In fact, Porphyry's point is precisely the one contained
in Macarius' reply: that the natural order cannot be overruled by the power
that created it.

[Matt. 4.6-7]

Yet another saying bears mentioning: It is where the tempter tells Jesus "Cast yourself down from the temple." But he does not do it, saying [to him] instead, "You shall not tempt the Lord your God." It looks as though he said this for fear of falling. If, as you say, Jesus worked other signs and even raised the dead by the power of his command, he certainly might have been willing to demonstrate that he could deliver others by first throwing himself down from the heights without hurting himself.

And this is the more true in view of another passage in the book, which says, "Their hands shall bear you up lest you dash your foot against a stone" [which the tempter himself cites]. The honest thing for Jesus to have done would be to demonstrate to those in the temple that he was God's son and was able to deliver them as well as himself from danger.[31]

---

31. Macarius argues against the probative value of the temptation sequence: Jesus was not concerned to demonstrate his power but to avoid acting in concert with the tempter. To have acceded to any one of his requests, even when they seemed to accord with prophecy, would have been to obey the power of evil.

6

The Attack on Peter the Apostle

Apocrit. III.19–III. 22

[Matt 16.23]
Nor is this the end of the inconsistencies that could be spelled out in relation to the gospels. The very words are at war with each other. One wonders, for example, how the man on the street would understand Jesus' rebuke of Peter, when he says, "Get behind me [you] Satan: you are an offense to me, for you care nothing for the things of God but only for the things of men."

But he says in a different mood, "You are Peter, and upon this rock will I build my church and I will give you the keys of the kingdom of heaven."

If [Jesus] thought so little of Peter as to call him a satan, worthy only to see his backside—an offense to him, and one who had no idea of the divinity [in his master]; and if he utterly rejected [Peter] as a sinner in the flesh—so much so that he did not want to look at his face any more—but cast him aside like a man condemned to banishment, how, I beg you tell me, is this curse on the so-called leader of the disciples to be interpreted?

Anyone with common sense who examines this passage and then hears Christ saying, "You are Peter and upon this rock will I build my church," and "I give to you the keys to the kingdom of heaven"—as though Jesus had forgotten his condemnation of Peter—anyone, I say, would laugh out loud until he could laugh no more. [Such a tale] would cause him to open his mouth as wide as he might in a theater and hiss and boo the players on stage, encouraging the audience to do the same.

Either [Jesus] was drunk with wine and not thinking clearly when he called Peter "Satan," or else when he promised [Peter] the keys to heaven he was deranged.

Tell us, how would Peter—a man of feeble judgment on innumerable occasions—be able to serve as the foundation of a church? What sort of sober reasoning do we see in him? Where does he show himself to be a man of discrimination and firm resolve? Perhaps when he is scared out of his wits by a young servant girl [who identifies him as a follower], and swears three times that he is not a disciple—just as [his master] said he would do? [Mark 14.69]

If Jesus was right in demeaning Peter by calling him "Satan," meaning one who is lacking every evidence of virtue, then [Jesus] proves himself inconsistent and lacking in foresight when he offers to Peter the leadership of the church.[32]

[Acts 5.1–11]
Peter is a traitor on other occasions: In the case of a man named Ananias and his wife, Sapphira, Peter put them to death

---

32. This is the beginning of a series of four attacks on the role of Peter in the gospels. Macarius deals with Porphyry's objections at the end of chapter xxvii, where the philosopher is accused of quoting verses out of context and in reverse order: the blessing on Peter occurs in Matt. 16.17-19 and is separate from the rebuke (16.22-23). Macarius suggests that Jesus does not identify Peter as the foundation or rock of the church ("*Su ei Petros*") but distinguishes him from the rock (*petra*) of divine teaching, upon which the church is built. With respect to the rebuke itself, Macarius offers that Jesus recognizes Satan speaking through Peter rather than Peter speaking of his own accord: "Knowing that the passion of Christ would be a liberation from the bonds of wickedness [Satan] was aiming to prevent the crucifixion." Macarius, however, does not deal with the more general criticism offered by Porphyry—namely that the gospel portrait of Peter is uncomplimentary and hence not befitting someone who is singled out for leadership.

for failing to surrender the profit from the sale of their land and retaining a little for their own use—even though they had done no [other wrong]. How can it have been wrong for them to retain a little of what belonged to them instead of giving it all away?

And even if [Peter] did think their actions wrong, he might have recalled Jesus' precepts, where he commands [believers] to endure 490 sins against them. Surely he could have pardoned the one sin, if a sin it was.

In his dealings with others, Peter should have remembered that he himself swore that he did not know Jesus and hence told a lie that demonstrated his complete contempt for the judgment and resurrection.[33]

[Acts 12.5-11; Gal. 2.12; 2 Cor. 11.13]
Among the company of disciples this man [Peter] ranked first. He had been taught by God to hate death, and escaping after being captured by Herod, he became the source of punishment for his captors. Once he had made his nighttime escape, there was a commotion at daybreak over how he had got out. When he failed to get any information from the guards upon questioning them, Herod ordered them to be taken away—that is, put to death.

And as I say, it is amazing that Jesus should have given the keys of the kingdom to a man like Peter. Why would he have commissioned a man so easily overwhelmed by fear, so confounded by difficulty such as [this one] to "Feed my lambs."[34]

---

33. Macarius claims in his response to the objection that Peter could not have forgiven Ananias and Sapphira their wrongdoing since their offense was against the whole body of believers, not just against an individual: "The outrage was committed against the deity, against the faith." He does not deal with the obvious parallel case, namely Peter's denial of Jesus, or with the absolution of that offense in John 21.15-18.

34. That Porphyry alludes to the passage in John 21.15ff. (see note 29 above) shows that he regards Jesus as mistaken in entrusting Peter with any administrative role. In political terms, Peter has shown only disloyalty and Jesus only poor judgment in forgiving and rewarding betrayal. The same view of the relationship between Jesus and his followers is held by Celsus (Hoffmann, *Celsus*, p. 66).

The sheep, I calculate, are those faithful perfected to the highest degree of the mystery, while the lambs are those still to be admitted and being fed the milk of [Christian] teaching.

Yet Peter is said to have been crucified after feeding the lambs only for a few months, even though Jesus had promised that the gates of hell would not devour him.[35]

Furthermore, Paul condemned Peter when he said, "Before certain men came from James, [Peter] ate with the gentiles, but when they came he separated himself, fearing those of the circumcision; and many of the Jews joined him in this hypocrisy." [Gal. 2.12] So here again we detect manifold error and contradiction: that a man entrusted with the interpretation of the divine words would behave so hypocritically with the intention of looking good to others.

The same can be said of [Peter's] hauling a wife about with him, as Paul reveals when he writes, "May we not take with us a sister, a wife—as do other apostles, and Peter" [1 Cor. 9.5]; or, as he adds, "Such are false apostles, deceitful workers" [2 Cor. 11.13]. That this same Peter holds the keys to heaven, looses and binds [sin] while being bound by sin

---

35. Although the tradition here cited is problematical, Crafer is probably correct in saying (p. 97, nn. 2, 3) that the boldness of the opponent's assertion suggests that it comes from Christian tradition. In fact, the Petrine tradition of Macarius' day was fluid. Eusebius quotes a certain Gaius of Rome and Dionysius of Corinth (*Ecclesiastical History* 3.1.2f.; 2.25.5-8) linking Peter with Rome and cites Origen to the effect that Peter was crucified head downward during the reign of Nero (54-68). St. Jerome attributed to Peter an episcopate of twenty-five years preceding his martyrdom, but the tradition is not well supported. Moreover Luke knows nothing of Peter's career extending beyond the early days of Paul's missionary work, and in fact the passage here singled out for scrutiny by the philosopher (Acts 12) is the last significant appearance of Peter in the Book of Acts. In Acts 21.18, James "the Just," also known as the brother of Jesus, appears as the sole authority in the Jerusalem church; no reference to Peter is made. The legend of Peter's further career and venture to Rome is a feature of a number of apocryphal books, notably the *Acts of Peter* composed in Syria ca. 200.

himself and immersed in hypocrisy, simply strikes terror in the heart.[36]

---

36. The passages from 1 Cor. 9.5. and 2 Cor. 11.13 are conflated by Porphyry to underscore the charge of hypocrisy contained in Gal. 2.12. The logic seems to be that Peter behaved hypocritically, both with respect to his relations with gentile believers and with respect to his marriage rights, which (contrary to the instruction contained in Mark 6.8-11) he seems to have insisted upon. The sense of this objection will have depended on the philosopher's endorsement of Paul's treatment of celibacy and self-mortification (e.g., 1 Cor. 9.27; 7.9, 32; Rom. 6.12, etc.), which Christian and gnostic teachers increasingly glossed in Platonic rather than in apocalyptic terms. On Peter's wife, cf. Mark 1.30. Paul's question explicitly reads: "*mē ouk echomen exousian adelphen gynaika periagein, hōs kai hoi loipoi apostoloi kai hoi adelphoi tou Kyriou kai Kephas?*," a liberal translation of which would be, "Do we not have the right to be accompanied by a sister-wife, as do the rest of the apostles and brothers of the Lord and Cephas [Peter]?"

7

The Attack on Paul the Apostle

Apocrit. III.30–III.36

[Acts 16.3]
[. . . You (Christians) seem to me to be like inexperienced sea-
farers, who while still afloat on one journey look ahead to
another voyage on another sea. And so you are looking for
other points to be put forward by us when you have not
completely answered questions already put to you.][37]

    How is it that Paul says, "Being free, I have made myself
the slave of all so that I might win all" [1 Cor. 9.19]; how,
even though he called circumcision "mutilation,"[38] he
nevertheless circumcised a certain man named Timothy, as

---

    37. The introductory remarks of iii.30 are those of Macarius rather than
his opponent and are contrived to extend the fiction of a dialogue. At this
point in the manuscript the word *hellene* is inserted as if to signal the point
at which the actual words of the philosopher begin. That Macarius thus
envelops the recorded words of his opponent for the sake of creating a sense
of drama, see Crafer's discussion, p. xvii. Harnack (p. 57) omits the
introductory material beginning with "*pōs ho Paulos elegteros gar on, legei*,
etc." ["How was it that Paul says. . . ?"].
    38. "*Pōs se kai tēn peritomēn legōn katatomēn. . . .*" The point seems
to be that Paul regarded circumcision as a mutilation of the flesh or of
no particular value. In fact, his comments in Phil. 3.2f. are more ambiguous
that Porphyry's reading suggests.

the Acts of the Apostles [16.3] instructs us. Ah! the asinine nature of all this. Such scenes are used in the theater in order to get a laugh. Jugglers give exhibitions like this! For how can a free man be everyone's slave?

How can someone so dependent as this gain anything? If he is an outlaw among the lawless who goes about with Jews as a Jew and with others as he pleases, then his slavery was service to his corruptness of nature, and he was a stranger to freedom. He is actually a slave and minister to the wrongdoing of others; he is an advocate of unhealthy things if he regularly squanders himself in serving people who have no law or accepts their actions as being the same as his own.

These are not the teachings of a healthy mind. This is not [the teaching] of unimpaired reason. The words indeed suggest someone who is mentally feeble and deficient in reasoning powers. And if he lives among the lawless yet accepts the religion of the Jews with an open heart, taking [as it were] a piece from each, then he is confused by each. He participates in their worst shortcomings and makes himself everyone's companion.

Anyone who makes circumcision the dividing line between believers and outsiders and then performs the ritual himself is his own worst accuser—as he says himself: "If I build again the things that I tore down, I make myself a transgressor."[39]

[Acts 22.3; Acts 22.27-9]
Paul also seems to forget himself frequently, as when he tells

---

39. With respect to Porphyry's generally high regard for the discipline of the Jewish law, see *Of Abstinence* 4.11-15. The philosopher seems to regard Paul's comments in 1 Cor. 9.19 less as a declaration of freedom from the law than as license to deal with converts dishonestly, as the need for persuasion warrants. Further, he tends to equate Paul's equivocal comments concerning gentile freedom from the law with "lawlessness" in the sense of moral anomie. Macarius argues that Paul behaved as a good teacher or doctor would, recognizing that the need to advance the gospel sometimes called for exceptional strategies—thus the circumcision of Timothy. Macarius sees no contradiction between Paul's expressed views toward circumcision and the account given by Luke in Acts 16.3 of Timothy's circumcision.

the captain of the guard that he is not a Jew but a Roman,[40] even though he had said on another occasion, "I am a Jew, born in Tarsus of Cilicia and raised up at the feet of Gamaliel, educated in accordance with the strict manner of the law of our fathers." [omitting *en tē polei tautē*]. But anyone saying [both] "I am a Jew" and "I am a Roman" is neither, even if he would like to be.

The man who hypocritically pretends to be what he is not makes himself a liar in everything that he does. He disguises himself in a mask. He cheats those who are entitled to hear the truth. He assaults the soul's comprehension by various tactics, and like any charlatan he wins the gullible over to his side.

Whoever accepts such principles as a guide for living cannot but be regarded as an enemy of the worst kind—the kind who brings others to submission by lying to them, who reaches out to make captives of everyone within earshot with his deceitful ways. And if, therefore, this Paul is a Jew one minute and the next a Roman, [or a student] of the [Jewish] law now, but at another time [an enemy of the law]—if, in short, Paul can be an enemy to each whenever he likes by burglarizing each, then clearly he nullifies the usefulness of each [tradition] for he limits their worthwhile distinctions with his flattery.

We may conclude that [Paul] is a liar. He is the adopted brother of everything false, so that it is useless for him to declaim, "I speak the truth in Christ, I do not lie" [Rom. 9.1];

---

40. The exact formulation attributed to Paul ("*Ego eimi anēr Ioudaios gegennemenos en Tarsō.* . . .") is taken to contradict the information supplied in Acts 22.27f., where Paul announces to the tribune that he was born (*gegennemai*) a citizen. Acts 21.40 represents him speaking to the people in Hebrew rather than in Greek (cf. 21.37). The account in the Book of Acts has always been problematical since nowhere in his letters does Paul claim Roman citizenship, and the degree of citizenship available to Jews living outside Rome is widely discussed. Here, however, neither Porphyry nor Macarius in his rebuttal regards citizenship as the issue. It is seen rather as an "ethnic" question, with Porphyry regarding Paul's claim to be Jewish as proof that he cannot have been a Roman, and Macarius responding that Paul's rejection by the Jews makes him an "honorary" Roman.

for a man who one day uses the law as his rule and the next day uses the gospel is either a knave or a fool in what he does in the sight of others and even when hidden away by himself.[41]

[1 Cor. 9.7]
[Paul] also misrepresents the gospel as his conceit requires, and uses the law for his own benefit: "Who serves as a soldier at his own expense, or who tends a herd without getting some of the milk?" And to get his portion, Paul invokes the law in support of his greed when he says, "Does not the law say the same, for it is written in the law of Moses, "You shall not muzzle an ox when it is treading out the grain' " [1 Cor. 9.9].

He adds next a piece of foolishness designed to limit God's providence to humanity and to deprive animals of the divine care: "Does God care about the oxen? Does he not speak entirely for our sake? It was written for our sake" [1 Cor. 9.10]. When he says such things, I think he makes the creator—who ages ago brought these [creatures] into being—look ridiculous, as though he had no concern [for his own creation].

For if it is true that God cares nothing for the oxen, why does scripture record, "He has made all things, sheep and oxen and beasts and birds and fishes, subject to him" [Ps. 8.8-9]. If [God] is concerned for fishes, then he must be all the more concerned for the toil of oxen! I am astonished at this man's pious regard for the law, since it is occasioned by his need to get donations from those who listen to his words.

[Rom. 7.12, 14]
Paul next turns around like a man startled awake by a nightmare, screaming, "I, Paul, testify that if a man keeps any bit of the law then he is indebted to the whole law." [Gal. 5.3, paraphrased; cf. James 2.10]. He says this rather than simply asserting that it is wrong to keep the commandments set down in the law.

---

41. The hypocrisy of Christian teachers was a feature of pagan polemic from at least the time of Celsus, who regards the charge as well established (Hoffmann, *Celsus,* p. 53).

A man whose intellectual powers are worthy of admiration—one instructed in the specifics of the law of his fathers,
one who frequently invokes the authority of Moses—is also
one, it seems, so sotted with wine that his wits have abandoned
him. Does [Paul] not erase the law for the sake of the Galatians
when he says, "Who bewitched you? How is it that you do
not obey the truth," which is the gospel [Gal. 3.1]? And as
if to press the point and make it an offense for anyone to
heed the law he says, "Those who are under the law are under
a curse" [Gal 3.10].

The same man who writes, "The law is spiritual" to the
Romans, and "The law is holy and the commandment holy
and just" now puts a curse upon those who obey what is holy!
Then, as if to confuse the point further, he turns everything
around and throws up a fog so dense that anyone trying to
follow him inevitably gets lost, bumping up against the gospel
on the one side, against the law on the other, stumbling over
the law and tripping over the gospel—all because the guide
who leads them by the hand has no idea where he is headed![42]

[Rom. 5.20]
Look again at this charlatan's record. Following any number
of references to the law which he used to find support [for his
case], he nullifies his argument by saying "The law entered so
that the offense might increase" and previous to this, "The goad
of death is sin and the power of sin is the law" [1 Cor. 15.56].

---

42. The philosopher shows a good deal of perception with respect to certain
inconsistencies in Paul's evaluation of the law and Paul's occasional appeals
to the law as a means of settling disputes. Macarius fairly represents the
complexity of the apostle's thought, however, when he responds, "If a man
keeps countless commandments and leaves only one undone, it is as bad as
leaving one gate of a city unprotected out of thirty-five" (iii.11). As to appeals
to the law (e.g., to Deut. 25.4 in 1 Cor. 9.9 or to Lev. 7.28 in 1 Cor. 9.13),
Macarius aptly responds that this is less an appeal than an allegorical
application of an Old Testament prototype; hence the law is "spiritual" or
"holy" as interpreted in the light of Christ's coming: "Is it for oxen that God
is concerned? Does he not speak entirely for our sake? It was written for
our sake."

With a tongue sharp as a sword, [Paul] mercilessly cuts the law into little pieces. But this is [nevertheless] the man who tends to keep the law and finds it virtuous to obey its commandments. By clinging to inconsistency, as he does apparently by habit, he overturns his judgments in all other cases.[43]

[1 Cor. 10.20-26; 8.4, 8]
Further, when Paul talks about eating what has been sacrificed to idols, his advice is essentially that it's all indifferent: [he tells his inquirers] not to ask too many questions, and that even though something has been a sacrifice to an idol, it can be eaten—just as long as no one tells them about it in advance! He says, in effect, "What they sacrifice they sacrifice to demons and I would not wish you to associate with demons."

But then he says, with indifference as to their dietary habits, "We know that an idol is nothing real, and that there is no God but one." Still later, "Food will not endear us to God: we are no worse off if we do not eat, and no better off if we do." Then following this prattle, [Paul] mutters like a man on his deathbed, "Eat whatever's sold in the meatmarket without raising questions on the basis of conscience, for the earth is the Lord's and everything in it."

How ridiculous this farce, based on nothing but the unparalleled inconsistency of his rantings! His sayings undercut

---

43. Neither Porphyry nor Macarius distinguishes between Paul's speculative use of the law (cf. Rom. 7.14) and his prudential use (e.g., Rom. 7.21ff.), and Paul at times blurs his own distinction, as in the passage cited (1 Cor. 15.56). This discussion is remarkable in that it centers on a controversy long settled by the fourth century and of no particular doctrinal importance. Even second-century writers had lost sight of the original context of Paul's concern over Christian freedom from the requirements of Jewish law (cf. 1 Tim. 1.8-9; James 2.18-26), preferring instead allegorical summaries such as the one provided by Macarius in chapter xli: the law is like the moon, drawing what light it has from the greater light of the sun, but destined to fade away as the sun reveals its glory. Like the moon, it has no power of its own, even though its place in the order of the universe is guaranteed.

each other as if by a sword. O brave new archery! that makes a target of the man who draws the bow![44]

[1 Tim. 4.1; 1 Cor. 7.25]
In letters written by him [Paul] gives us to believe that virginity is to be praised. Then he turns around and says, "In these last days some will depart from the faith and will find themselves swayed by seducing spirits who forbid them to marry and command them to abstain from meat" [1 Tim 4.1, 3]. But then, in his letter to the Corinthians, he says, "But with regard to virgins I have no commandment of the Lord."

Thus, anyone who remains single is not doing the right thing—and anyone who refrains from marriage as though it were evil is not acting in accordance with [the commandments of Jesus], since there is no record of Jesus' words concerning virginity. What about those people who brag of being virgins

---

44. According to Acts 15, Paul and Barnabas are sent as delegates to gentile populations in Antioch, Syria and Cilicia with an apostolic decree to the effect that the congregations abstain from eating meat obtained through pagan sacrifice. Porphyry does not deal with the contradictions between the information provided by Luke and Paul's cautious endorsement of freedom of conscience with respect to the dietary practices of gentile converts. In his rebuttal Macarius refers his opponent to his own words in the *Peri tēs ek Logiōn Philosophiās* (*The Philosophy from Oracles*), which serves as his sourcebook for information concerning the sacrifices of the mystery cults. Crafer mistakenly concludes (p. xiv; p. 111, n. 1) that this referral counts against Harnack's belief that the writer of the objections is Porphyry himself. On the contrary, it is obvious in context that Macarius is toying with his opponent and in this instance taunting him with his own book; thus, "You may learn accurately the record of the things sacrificed when you read the oracle of Apollo concerning sacrifices, handed down to the initiates in a mystery [recounted] by Porphyry in his arrogant delight, [where they are bound] by a terrifying oath [not to tell] the mystery to the people. The tragic result of this new superstition *would be well known to you . . .*" [emphasis mine]. It seems to me very likely that this response, replete as it is with Macarius' citing his opponent's words from an established source, is one of the surest evidences that the opponent is indeed Porphyry.

as if they were singled out to be filled with the holy spirit, as was the mother of Jesus.[45]

---

45. Porphyry's objection is based on his generally high regard for sexual abstinence. He appears to know that Paul's argument in 1 Cor. applies to unmarried men as well as to women and is linked to Paul's eschatological teaching rather than to gnostic or neoplatonic pessimism. As a pupil of Plotinus, Porphyry would have been in sympathy with his teacher's correction of Platonic philosophy on this point (e.g., 2 *Ennead* 9.17-18), and thus may have been in sympathy with Paul's view that sexual abstinence is a provisional mode of conduct entailed by "the present distress" (1 Cor. 7.26-31) rather than a means of expressing the doctrine that the corporeal is inferior to the spiritual. In the *Letter to His Wife Marcella*, Porphyry writes that "it is a great proof of wisdom to hold the body in thrall; often men cast off certain parts of the body; be ready for the soul's safety to cast the whole body away." (*Letter* 29-34, pp. 56-59). In view of the traditional acquaintance of Origen and Porphyry, the reference to "cutting" or casting away parts of the body may refer to the Christian teacher's castration, carried out in accordance with a reading (or misreading) of Matt. 19.12. Neither Porphyry nor Macarius would have been aware that the view represented in 1 Tim. is a later writer's effort to improve Paul's views on virginity. Without the contradiction, the objection fails.

Macarius turgid response argues that, as virginity is an *unnatural* state, it is left for the individual to choose it, with greater merit arising from its being a matter of choice than if it were made compulsory. The heretics envisaged in 1 Tim. 4.1f. would have made it the latter, and so would have deprived chastity or sexual abstinence of its value.

8

The Attack on
Christian Apocalyptic Hopes

Apocrit. IV.1–IV.7

[I Cor. 7.31]
What can Paul mean when he says that the form [*skēma*] of this world is passing away? And how can those who have [possessions] act as though they had nothing, or those who are satisfied—how can they not be? How can the other fables [he recounts] be believed? How is the form of this world to pass away—or more precisely, *what* is it that passes away and why does it do so?

For if the creator is the cause of its passing away he would be guilty of causing something securely established to change. And even if he could change its form for the better, he would nonetheless be guilty of ignorance in failing to provide a permanent and suitable form for the world at the time of its creation, and of making instead an imperfect mess [of his work].[46]

---

46. This represents a continuation of the critique of Paul's teaching, but thematically it is centered on Christian belief in the *parousia*, or second coming, and attendant signs of judgment and resurrection. The idea that the creator had made a "mess" of his work recalls Marcion's objections to the work of the demiurge: cf. Tertullian, *Against Marcion* 1.28. In the same section Tertullian takes up the question of abstinence—also highly regarded by the

More to the point, one cannot know that the world would be changed from bad to good at the end of time; hence, what would be the good result of rearranging the parts? If it's the way of the world to be a source of misery, it must be objected— so loudly that the creator will cup his ears at the protest— that he is the whole source of the misery and grief: he is the source of the problem. It is he who violates the rationality of nature, he who must repent for botching things, and he who must choose to patch up the holes in the wall of his own creation.[47]

Marcionite Christians—arguing in familiar fashion that "commendation given to abstinence is of no account when prohibition is imposed" (1.29).

47. This is an echo of a familiar criticism leveled at Christian belief (cf. Hoffmann, *Celsus*, pp. 101-103). Porphyry's high regard for the rationality of the created order derives from Plotinus (2 *Ennead* 10, 13, esp. 9.8): "The universe is a life organized, effective, complex, all-comprehensive, displaying an unfathomable wisdom. How then can anyone [viz., the "gnostics"] deny that it is a clear image, beautifully formed, of the Intellectual Divinities? No doubt it is a copy, not original; but that is its very nature; it cannot be at once a symbol and reality. But to say that it is an inadequate copy is false. Nothing has been left out which a beautiful representation within the physical order could include."

Macarius in his reply completely misses the eschatological issue at stake in Paul's comment and Porphyry's criticism. Working from the Jewish perspective of his day, Paul could only reject the proto-gnostic views of some Christian communities, who were attracted to a more pronounced form of dualism than Paul felt able to embrace. The Epistle to the Romans, for example, is written in the interest of preserving the theoretical value of Jewish law within the Christian context of fulfillment (cf. Rom. 13.10), whereas gnostic and Marcionite teachers thought of the law in terms of antithesis and dichotomy—the old supplanted by the new, or the inferior and known superseded by the superior and unknown (cf. Tertullian, *Against Marcion* 1.2-6). Paul's eschatological perspective does not issue in a condemnation of the created order: the world is a visible symbol of the "eternal power and divine nature" (Rom. 1.19-20). By the same token, this world is "passing away" (Rom. 13.11-12). It is difficult to trace anything in Paul's thought comparable to Porphyry's high estimate of the orderliness of the connative world. Macarius is even further from Paul's logic than his opponent, however, in suggesting that Paul is speaking of the passing "fashions" of the world rather than about the end of time.

Perhaps Paul means to say that the wealthy should behave as though their money were of no account—since the creator—in speeding the world toward its end—acts as though it were not his possession. And perhaps Paul means that those who are satisfied should act as though they were not—in the sense that the creator seems not to be satisfied when he gazes upon the beauty of what he has made, but instead grieves over it as though it were not beautiful. And so he gets on with his plan to remodel the house, the easier to pass it off to someone else.

[1 Thess. 4.15-17]
Another of his astonishingly silly comments needs to be examined: I mean that wise saying of his, to the effect that, "We who are alive and persevere shall not precede those who are asleep when the Lord comes; for the Lord himself will descend from heaven with a shout, with the voice of an archangel; and the trumpet of God shall sound, and those who have died in Christ shall rise first; then we who are alive shall be caught up together with them in a cloud to meet the Lord in the air; and so we shall be forever with the Lord."

Indeed—there is something here that reaches up to heaven: the magnitude of this lie. When told to dumb bears, to silly frogs and geese—they bellow or croak or quack with delight to hear of the bodies of men flying through the air like birds or being carried about on clouds. This belief is quackery of the first rank: that the weight of our mortal flesh should behave as though it were of the nature of winged birds and could navigate the winds as easily as ships cross the sea, using clouds for a chariot! Even if such a thing could happen, it would be a violation of nature and hence completely unfitting.

For the nature which is begotten in all things from the beginning also assigns to those things a certain station and rank in the order of the universe:[48] the sea for creatures that

---

48. The source of this objection derives from Plotinus' theory of the divisibility of the soul as a fragmented and widely repeated image of the soul-in-unity: 4 *Ennead* 8-9; cf. 2 *Ennead* 1-2. Christian writers such as Paul had made use of miscellaneous Hellenistic models in reaching for a coherent view of the resurrection of the dead at the eschaton; see note following.

thrive in water; the land for creatures who thrive on ground; the air for the creatures who have wings; the reaches of the heavens for the celestial bodies. Move one creature from its appointed place to another sphere and it will die away in its strange abode. "You can't take a fish out of water," for it will surely die on the dry land. Just the same, you can't hope to make land animals creatures of the sea: they will drown. A bird will die if it is deprived of its habitat in the air, and you cannot make a heavenly body an earthly one.[49]

The divine and active *logos* [word] of God has never tampered with the nature of things and no god ever shall, even though the power of God can affect the fortunes of created things. God does not work contrary to nature: he does not flaunt his ability but heeds the suitability of things [to their environment, in order to] preserve the natural order. Even if he could do so, God would not cause ships to sail across the continents or cause farmers to cultivate the sea. By the same token, he does not use his power to make evildoing an act of goodness nor turn an act of charity into an evil deed. He does not turn our arms into wings and he does not place the earth above the stars. Therefore, a reasonable man can only conclude that it is idiotic to say that "Men will be caught up . . . in the air."

And there is more to Paul's lying: He very clearly says,

---

49. Compare this to Paul's language in 1 Cor. 15.39-45. The Greeks had no difficulty in conceiving of the immortality of the soul, but the idea of a raised body was difficult. Paul had tried to strike a compromise by saying that the resurrection will respect the natural order, within which there are diverse "kinds" of bodies; hence, the resurrected body would be a new and imperishable one. The philosopher's point is directed against this premise. On Plotinus' view of the organization of souls, which forms the basis for Porphyry's discussion, see 4 *Ennead* 3.15-16: Of the "variation of bodies entered by souls," he comments that "they live by the code of the aggregate of beings, the code which is woven out of the Reason-Principles and all other causes ruling in the Cosmos, out of the soul movements and out of the laws springing in the Supreme; a code, therefore, consonant with those higher existences, founded upon them, keeping unshakably true all that is capable of holding itself set toward the divine nature, and leading round by all appropriate means whatsoever is less natively apt" [15b].

"*We* who are alive." For it is now three hundred years since he said this and nobody—not Paul and not anyone else—has been caught up in the air. It is high time to let Paul's confusions rest in peace![50]

---

50. A literal interpretation of the philosopher's words at this point would place the writing at around 350 C.E.—given a traditional dating for Paul's correspondence with the Thessalonian church (ca. 51 C.E.). Of course there is no reason to suppose that Porphyry himself knew anything of the chronology of the letters and is doubtless guessing at a plausible date based on what he may have known of traditions about Paul's life or the time of his death. Crafer observes (p. xvii) "a round number does not count for much—especially in days before time was reckoned in the Christian era."

If the date is exaggerated in any direction, then in the service of his point (i.e., that three full *centuries* have passed without Christian hopes materializing) it is obviously on the long side. In this case, the sentence may be read colloquially as "The best part of three centuries has passed since Paul wrote this."

The bearing of the reading on authorship, however, should not be overlooked. Porphyry became Plotinus' disciple in 263, about seven years before his teacher's death in Campania. The collecting and organizing of Plotinus' works seems to have begun straightaway. Porphyry died in 303, a date which suggests that his treatise against the Christians would have been completed toward the end of his philosophical career. The Göttingen professor Magnus Crusius (cf. J.-P. Migne, *Patrologia Graeca* 10: 1343f.) argued for a date toward the beginning of the fourth century. And the French Roman Catholic scholar Louis Duchesne (*De Macario Magnete et scriptis eius* [Paris: Klincksieck, 1877]) places the *Apocriticus* itself at the beginning of the fourth century. Duchesne, however, saw the pagan objections as coming from a "lesser man" than Porphyry, namely his disciple, the neoplatonist Hierocles.

Against the idea that Hierocles rather than Porphyry is the author of the objections (cf. Crafer, p. xiii) is the fact that Hierocles is not known to have written a tract "against" the Christians, but rather two books titled *The Friend of Truth* (*Philalētheis Logoi*; cf. Lactantius, *Divine Institutes* 5.2) intended for their instruction. As a contemporary of Porphyry, Lactantius (d. 320) was in a position to know the differences in style, tenor and substance of the two works. Eusebius, moreover, describes the work of Porphyry as "an attempt to slander the sacred scriptures" and indicts his efforts for showing a lack of philosophical argument (*Ecclesiastical History* 6.19.2-3). The strongly anti-Origenist and anti-allegorical twist of Porphyry's line of argument may have something to do with Eusebius' claim that Porphyry

[Matt. 24.14]

On the same subject, there is a saying given by Matthew. It is as servile a piece of work as ever came from a drudge in a factory: "The Gospel of the kingdom shall be preached in all the world, and then the end will come."⁵¹ Consider that every corner of the world has heard of the gospel; that everyone—everywhere—has the finished product—but that the end has not come and will never come. This saying should be whispered, not said aloud!⁵²

---

as a young man had met and listened to Origen and developed a dislike for his teaching. Origen died in 254 when Porphyry would have been about twenty-two, so the possibility of their meeting is not remote. Slanders against Origen, alleged by Eusebius as a feature of Porphyry's writing, have been removed or omitted by Macarius.

A further issue is the suggestion that the polemic was written considerably *later* than the objections of the philosopher. Crafer has argued persuasively that, "If Macarius is writing a long time after Christianity has ceased to be an unlawful religion [i.e., if this Macarius is a fifth-century bishop of Magnesia who attended the synod of Oak in 403] why should he adopt such a trembling attitude before his opponent and need to brace himself continually against a nameless dread which nearly overwhelmed him?" (p. xvii)

In short, it is far more likely that the pagan and Christian are near contemporaries than that the ideas of a pagan philosopher should be dredged up for ridicule in the fifth century, by which time most of the philosophical criticisms would seem stale and tangential to the main lines of post-Nicene controversy. By the same token, there is no reason to think that Macarius was not working from an epitome of the *Kata Christianōn* rather than from the books themselves, though a likelier solution in my view is that he is far more selective in manipulating his opponent's work than Origen was in his treatment of Celsus' *Alēthēs Logos*.

In the passage quoted from 1 Thess., Porphyry wishes to remind the Christians of the empirical "disconfirmation" of their early apocalyptic hopes. The ploy is lost in the Origenist interpretation given by Macarius, who suggests that Paul's confident assertion, "We who are alive . . ." shows only that "he is fond of identifying his own humanity with that of the whole race."

51. Porphyry abbreviates the text of Matt. 24.14.

52. The substance of this saying is not of much help in dating the philosopher's writing, since Tertullian could already make exaggerated claims

Acts 18.9-10]
Let us see what Paul was told: "The Lord said to Paul at night in a vision, 'Do not be afraid: speak, for I am with you, and no one will pounce on you to harm you.' " But as soon as [Paul] was taken prisoner in Rome, the very same—who had said that we shall judge the angels—had his head cut off! So, too, Peter, who was given the duty to feed the lambs [John 21.17] was nailed to a cross and then impaled for display. Many others of the same opinions have been burned, scourged, or otherwise put to death as punishment [for their teachings]. But it is not befitting the will of God—nor even the wishes of a good man—that thousands should be tortured for their beliefs while the time of his coming and their reward [resurrection] remains unknown.[53]

---

for the growth of the church at the end of the second century (e.g., *Apology* 50). Macarius recites a list of people to whom the gospel has not yet been preached, including "seven races of the Indians who live in the southeastern desert, and the Macrobians of Ethiopia." The philosopher doubtless means the Roman world, divided between east and west, while the Christian writer reaches into Herodotus for details.

A writer of around the year 300 could be expected to comment on the extent of the appeal and success of Christianity and to employ the growing political confidence of the new religion as a contrast to its original apocalyptic interests. Macarius' defense against this "reminder" is to challenge the philosopher's interpretation of the word *telos* (end), as Matthew uses it, and to give it a more philosophical twist: the end (*telos*) God desires is the end of wickedness through the preaching of the Gospel. Theoretically, there is no literal end to such an enterprise until it can be shown that wickedness has been conquered once and for all. Until this happens, the "end" in its eschatological sense cannot come. "And so God in his mercy prorogues the cycle of time which moves toward an end." The logic represented by Macarius is ultimately that which informs the imperial ecclesiology of the later fourth century.

53. Porphyry's logic is oblique in this passage. Essentially he is continuing a digression on the apocalyptic expectations of Christianity, and here his approach is to use passages from scripture antithetically in relation to extracanonical traditions. Thus Paul, who was "emboldened to speak by a promise of immunity from harm," died the death of a martyr nonetheless. Peter was curtailed as well in his efforts to preach the gospel.

[Matt. 24.4-5]
In another place there is a slippery little saying attributed to
Christ when he says, "Be on guard, so that no one will deceive
you: for many will come in my name saying, 'I am Christ'
and [they] will deceive many."

And see: more than three hundred years on, no one of the
sort has appeared anywhere. Unless, of course, you are going
to throw up the case of Apollonius of Tyana, that paragon
of philosophy. But there is no other, and in any case [Jesus]
predicts not that one but that many such Christs would arise.[54]

According to a late second-century work, *The Acts of Paul*, the apostle
was martyred on the left bank of the Tiber three miles outside Rome. The
place, known as Ad Aqua Salvias, was renamed Tre fontana, from the legend
that when Paul's head bounced three times, three fountains sprang forth.
Tradition locates his death in the Neronian persecution, ca. 65; Tertullian
adds the detail—apparently widely accepted—that he was beheaded
(*Prescription against Heretics* 36).

For the philosopher the deaths of the martyrs are not testimonies to
their courage or the solidity of their belief in the resurrection of the dead.
Rather, they are proof that Christian teaching runs contrary to the will of
God, since he seems to act as an adversary to their cause. Further, he does
not offer them the satisfaction of knowing when he might bring persecution
to an end.

Whether these persecutions are contemporary (or nearly so) with the
philosopher's objections cannot be determined. In 303—the year of Porphyry's
death—Diocletian initiated the "Great Persecution" at the urging of Galerius
and Porphyry's disciple Hierocles.

54. It is not clear that the philosopher understands the context of the
saying in Matthew's gospel, where the point is to distinguish false messiahs
from the true Christ. In any case, Porphyry does not credit the saying since
he does not find it borne out by historical evidence. It follows for him that
if *no* false Christs have appeared (Apollonius of Tyana being the named
exception), then the proliferation of messianic claims cannot be used to
exonerate Christian beliefs about the end of history.

Macarius offers in rebuttal an unlikely assortment of names—from Manes
of Persia to Montanus, Marcion, and Dositheus of Cilicia—as messianic
pretenders and antichrists. It is not clear whether Macarius takes the point
that the coming of false messiahs was linked to the imminence of the second
coming of Jesus and the judgment of the world. Porphyry seems to suggest
that no one making precisely the *same messianic claims* as Jesus has come.

[*Apocalypse of Peter*]
There are plenty of other statements [regarding this cataclysm expected by the Christians]. In the *Apocalypse of Peter* [he] says that heaven will be judged along with the earth: "The earth will belch forth all the dead on the day of God's judgment, and it shall be judged together with the heaven which contains it."[55] Is anyone so illiterate, so dim, that he does not know that earthly things [alone] are subject to disturbance and do not behave in such a way as to maintain their existence and order but are, rather, erratic in their movement.

The things of heaven, on the other hand, possess an order that belongs entirely to them and is always the same. It maintains itself in perfect harmony [by the divine will]; it never changes and it will never be other than what it is.

[This order] is God's masterwork of precision. And since all that exists is as it is by virtue of the divine ordinance, it is impossible that the order of creation can be other than what it is; no better order can be conceived for it.

Further: why would heaven be *judged*? Will you tell us that once upon a time it committed some great sin—even though it manifests the order declared for it by God and does not and has never suffered any alteration in its movement? Or perhaps you will tell us that it is enough for the creator to

---

Celsus had offered the related objection that the prophecies used by the Christians in support of their messianic beliefs could be applied to any one of dozens of pretenders to the title of messiah (cf. Hoffmann, *Celsus*, p. 58).

55. The work referred to dates from the first half of the second century and is mentioned by Clement of Alexandria, who regarded it as authentic, and by Eusebius (*Ecclesiastical History* 6.14.1) who regards it as a forgery. It remained one of the most popular apocryphal writings until its definitive exclusion from Athanasius' canon of 367. Undoubtedly Porphyry thinks of the book as canonical. It includes both the text of Matt. 24.5 (the reference to false Christs) as well as a vivid description of the melting of the heavens on the day of judgment (*Apocalypse of Peter* 5). The philosopher quotes accurately from the source, that heaven and earth will be judged together, and seems also to know the tradition of Isa. 34.4, that "heaven shall be rolled up like a fig tree." The objection to these images of destruction is paraphrased from Plotinus' theory of the permanence of the heavenly order, 2 *Ennead* 1.4.

interfere with the [orderly operation of the heavens] on a whim, spewing curses at his own handiwork—wonderful and great as it is.[56]

[Isa. 34.4]
And the sacred word used [by the Christians] slanderously asserts that "all the power of heaven will melt away, and heaven will be rolled up like a scroll, and the stars will fall like leaves from the vine, as leaves fall from a fig tree." To make the lie fouler than it already smells, [Matthew] says, "Heaven and earth will pass away but my words will not pass away." Odd, is it not, to imagine that the words of Jesus would still be heard if there were no heaven and earth to contain them? And if Christ should do this—bring heaven down—then he would be acting like the worst of sinners, those who murder their own children, since the Son admits that God is the father of heaven and earth when he says, "Father: Lord of heaven and earth" [Matt. 11.25].

And the baptizer John praises heaven and the gifts that come from heaven when he says, "A man can accomplish nothing unless it is given to him from heaven" [John 3.27]. And the prophets say that heaven is the habitation of God, writing, "Look down from your holy habitation [heaven] and bless your people Israel" [Deut. 26.15].

If, therefore, heaven is of such great importance, as the testimony of scripture would suggest, where shall its ruler live after it passes away? Where shall be his throne? And if the earth perishes, where will God put his feet, since he

---

56. The passage has suffered some mutation and cannot be translated satisfactorily as it now appears in the text. Crafer's attempt to render the passage (p. 130, n. 1) is unsatisfactory. On the probable source of Porphyry's argument cf. Plotinus, 2 *Ennead* 4.5.

says, "The heaven is my throne and the earth is the footstool of my feet." So much for the passing away of heaven and earth![57]

---

57. Porphyry's tactic is to take Christian imagery in its most literal sense. If heaven and earth pass away, then God would have no dwelling place. This subject is never broached in Christian apocalyptic thought, which chose instead to emphasize the creation of a "new heaven and a new earth" (Isa. 65.17).

Macarius responds to the objections by identifying the *logoi* referred to by Jesus in Matt. 24.35 with the Stoical *logos* which provides the reason or rationale for the created order; thus, "all created things that come to an end do so to achieve a second and better beginning."

9

The Kingdom of Heaven and the Obscurity of Christian Teaching

Apocrit. IV.8–IV.19

[Matt. 13.31–33, 45–46]
Turning to consider another doctrine, one even more astonishing than the others and just as obscure, we find this [written]: "The kingdom of heaven is like a grain of mustard seed" or, "The kingdom of heaven is like leaven" or, "The kingdom of heaven is like a merchant seeking pearls of value."

These wild images are not the work of wise men nor even of the sibyls. When someone wants to say something concerning the realm of the divine, it is necessary for him to make his point clearly using everyday images. But these images are not commonplace: they are degraded and unintelligible. They are unfit to convey the intended comparison. They make no sense.

But it was necessary that they should be clear, since they were intended not for the wise or understanding—but for babes [cf. 1 Cor. 3.1; Matt. 11.25].[58]

---

58. The philosopher equates references to the kingdom of heaven or kingdom of God with heaven. The Jewish context of the phrase, and presumably that which made its way into early Christian belief, saw "kingdom" as the exercise of God's power at the time of judgment—an event ascribed to the immediate future in some texts (e.g., Mark 9.1; Matt. 25.31,

[Matt. 11.25]
Jesus says on another occasion, "I thank you, Father, Lord of heaven and earth, because you have hid these things from the wise and prudent and revealed them to babes." And it is written in the Book of Deuteronomy, "The hidden things for the Lord our God, the manifest for us" [Deut. 29.29]. It is obvious [to a wise man] that what is written for the babes and the ignorant should be clear and not covered with riddles: but if the mysteries hidden from the wise are offered in turn to suckling babes, then [it would seem] better to be stupid and senseless. And is this the great contribution of that all-wise [one] who came to earth—that the light of knowledge should be hidden from the wise but revealed to fools and babies?

[Matt. 9.12; Luke 5.21]
By contrast I mention now another item of a more reasonable sort—namely the saying, "They that are well need no physician but rather those who are sick." Christ reveals this to a crowd with respect to his [reason for] coming to earth. If, as he says, he confronted sin for the sake of those who are weak, what of our forefathers, our ancestors—were they not likewise

---

etc.). In liturgical formulae (cf. 1 Cor. 16.22) and New Testament apocalyptic traditions attributed to Jesus (Mark 13.24–36) these events are greeted with enthusiasm. The images of leaven, mustard seed, grain, hidden pearls, etc., are entirely appropriate to the earliest—and especially the persecutionist— phase of Christian belief, but they seem inept to the philosopher. It appears to him that Christians no longer take such images seriously, and he finds vacuous their attempts to allegorize away previous expectations. If the images are not indicative of an historical process, therefore, they must, he thinks, be understood spatially. Understood in this way, however, they become philosophically vulnerable to neoplatonic criticism that the cosmos and its creator (the Demiurge or, colloquially, Zeus for Plotinus) is a principle of unchanging order and unity, without cessation (4 *Ennead* 4.11).

Macarius does what he can in his reply by insisting that the mustard seed is not an image of impending judgment, but shows the relation of the earth to heaven. The objection and its rebuttal show that by the beginning of the fourth century both the pagan critics of the Christian church and Christian teachers had some trouble responding to historical context, and hence to the original meaning of Matt. 13.36–50.

diseased and weakened by sin? Those who are whole [he says] need no physician. He came [he says] not to call the righteous but sinners, as Paul also claims when he says, "Jesus Christ came into the world to save sinners, of which I am one of the greatest" [1 Tim. 1.5].

If this is true, that those who have gone astray are called, and those who are diseased are healed, while the unrighteous [are] called and the righteous [are] not—then it follows that the one who is neither called nor in need of healing among the Christians would be a righteous man who had not gone astray. That is: he who needs no healing [is precisely] the man who turns his back on the word of faith; and the more he turns away from it the more righteous and whole he is and the less he goes astray.[59]

[I Cor. 6.11]
Homer elicits a practiced silence from the Greeks when he

---

59. The searing logic of this passage evokes a muddled response from Macarius, who quickly becomes entangled in an allegorical interpretation of verses only vaguely related to the objection in its original context. Matt. 9.12 refers to a confrontation between Jesus and the Pharisees over an apparent violation of Jewish purifactory laws and table fellowship. The antithetical use of *dikaios* and *hamartolos* (righteous/sinner) is probably intended ironically: the "righteous" who complain of breaches of the law evidently have no need of further instruction, whereas sinners clearly do: hence, Jesus' association with sinners.

All of this is lost on Porphyry and missed by the ingenuity of Macarius' reply. For the philosopher, Jesus' words connote that it would be better to *reject* the message of the gospel, since continuing as a sinner promotes the efforts required for righteousness and spiritual well-being. Accepting the word identifies one as a sinner and "saves" the person from the condition of sinfulness through no obvious effort of his own. Macarius argues that the "righteous" are the angels "whose pure and immutable nature requires nothing in the way of repentance from them," while the sinner and the sick are the race of men "whose glory was equal to that of the angels in the beginning." In his letter to Marcella, Porphyry emphasizes that "mere unreasoning faith without right living does not attain to God. Nor is it an act of piety to honor God without having first ascertained in what manner he delights to be honored" (*Letter to Marcella* 22).

tells of Hector's declamation: "Hold fast, Argives; lift not a hand, you Achaean boys: for Hector with his waving plume has something to say." Just so, we all sit in silence here, because the Christian teacher has promised that he will unlock for us the dark mysteries of scripture.[60]

So, dear sir: tell us what the Apostle means when he says, "But such were some of you" (that is, something wretched).[61] But, he goes on, "You were washed, you were sanctified, you were justified in the name of the Lord Jesus Christ and in the spirit of our God." It is indeed troubling and confusing to think that a man, once washed of so much pollution and rot, seems [all of a sudden] to be pure. [Is it not a little curious], this wiping away the stains of a lifetime of immorality—of sexual license, adultery, drunkenness, thieving, perversions,

---

60. Omitted is an incipit supplied by Macarius in the interest of preserving the dialogue format. The style would suggest that Macarius is quoting verbatim from the philosopher's book. Macarius has argued that "certain words of Homer" were introjected into the debate for ridicule— probably with the intention of presenting the objections as interrogatories in a case at law, intended to evoke serious responses from the Christians. A useful comparison is the format of the *Octavius* of Minucius Felix, written in the late second (?) century as a discussion between Octavius, a Christian, and the pagan Caecilius. Macarius' *Apocriticus* lacks the systematic structure of the earlier, highly artificial work. Moreover, the rhetorical flourishes against the Christian teacher show signs of the "slanderous" style with which Eusebius associates Porphyry's attack (*Ecclesiastical History* 6.19.2).

This said, it is doubtful in my view that the teacher so addressed is Macarius. In all probability, the "dialogue" is written in the form of an interrogation, as Celsus' had been, with a silent (or dumbfounded) Christian sitting in the hypothetical dock. Throughout this portion of the treatise, it is notable that Macarius exhibits neither the systematic logic of Minucius Felix nor the theological dexterity of Origen. The objections do not seem to be stylized on the Christian side, but on the pagan, where the original "slanderous intent" of the philosopher has been preserved. Macarius is only rarely able to meet the objections head on.

61. The full passage reads, "Neither the immoral, nor idolaters, nor adulterers, nor sexual perverts, nor thieves, nor the greedy, nor drunkards, nor revilers, nor robbers will inherit the Kingdom of God. And such were some of you" (1 Cor. 6.9–11).

self-abuse—and assorted disgusting things—simply by getting baptized, or calling on the name of Christ to get free of sin, as easily as a snake sloughs off its old skin?

I ask, who wouldn't prefer a life of corruption, based on the strength of these [promises]; who would not choose a life of evildoing and unutterable wickedness if he knew in advance that all would be forgiven him if only he believed and was baptized, confident in his heart that the judge of the living and the dead would pardon any offense he had committed. Such [promises] encourage those who hear them to sin; and the teaching of such a doctrine produces an attitude of disobedience. [Further] such a doctrine tends to supersede training in the virtue of obedience, so that doing what is right becomes indistinct and ineffective in relation to what is wrong.

[The Christians] would bring us a society without law. They would teach us to have no fear of the gods. This arrogant saying says as much in asserting that the whole range of our wrongdoing can be washed away just by being baptized.[62]

---

62. On the practice of baptism as a means of "washing away" wrongdoing, see especially Tertullian, *Of Baptism* 15. In Porphyry's day the penitential system which compensated for sins committed after Christian baptism had not yet developed. The practice of "clinical" baptism—that is, the postponement of baptism until old age or illness made it advisable, in view of its effectiveness against sin—was common in the fourth century. Clinical baptism was considered inferior to "regular" baptism, and those thus baptized incurred an impediment barring them from the priesthood if they recovered from their illness.

Porphyry seems to object to the casual concern exhibited by some Christians toward sin and forgiveness. He sees Paul advocating an abdication of moral responsibility. In fact Paul seems to have viewed baptism as a "pledge" of new life in which God's grace would be expressed in the condition of responsibly exercised moral freedom (1 Cor. 6.12) rather than restriction and law.

The philosopher singles out that portion of Paul's theology of baptism which informs the sacramental theology of the fourth century and climaxes in Augustine's treatises, *De baptismo contra Donatistas*, ca. 400, and *De unico baptismo contra Petilianum*, ca. 410. Both treatises have to do with heretical baptism, but in more general terms with the "effectiveness" and "operation" of the sacrament.

Macarius regards the grace conferred in baptism as a "reprieve from death," issued by a monarchial God who possesses sole power to pardon wrongdoing and offense. This forgiveness is regarded as an illustration of the benevolence, mercy, wisdom, or "princely virtue" of the monarch, and never as a necessity entailed by the action, petition, or performance of the wrongdoer. Thus, when granted, forgiveness "glorifies the pardoner [whose] deed is made to shine forth as a gift of grace, so that it is not ascribed to the [merit of the sinner]." As to the effect of the sacrament, the baptismal water is regarded as "immeasurably potent and able to wash away not only the dirt of the physical body, but penetrates even the parts of the conscience that are hidden and purifies them."

The answer is wayward at times; Macarius argues that each of the persons of the divine trinity is individually able to provide the sanctification attributed to the Holy Spirit. Insofar as his reply touches on the main point of the philosopher's objection—namely, that a "high" theology of baptism may encourage moral lassitude—Macarius says nothing to obviate the problem.

Porphyry acknowledges the importance of prayers of thanksgiving, since ingratitude to God is a moral wrong. He finds offense, however, in the Christian idea that prayer and sacrifice (eucharist) might compel God to respond to prayer in a particular way. Broadly speaking, doxological prayer (thanksgiving or glorification) were commended by Platonizing Christian teachers like Origen, while supplicatory prayer was seen as compromising belief in the divine impassibility and immutability. Gen. 6.6 was used both by heretics like Marcion and by pagan observers to point up the inadequacy of the creator's rule and consistency.

10

The Christian Doctrine of God

Apocrit. IV.20-IV.23

Let us explore completely this matter of the monarchy of the only God and the manifold rule [polyarchy] of those who are revered as gods. Your idea of the single rule [monarchy] is amiss, for a monarch is not the only man alive but the only man who rules.[63]

He rules, obviously, over his kinsmen and those like himself. Take for example the emperor Hadrian: he was a monarch because he ruled over those who were like him by race and nature—not because he existed alone somewhere or lorded it over oxen and sheep, as some poor shepherd might

---

63. That is, he does not share power and no one is capable of overthrowing him. His rule, however, presupposes the existence of others like him in all ways except with respect to his *monarchia*, that is, the power that is uniquely his. In the second and third centuries, the term *monarchy* was employed as a synonym for the unity of the godhead. Western theologians tended to emphasize monarchy as a defense against the charge of polytheism on the one side and atheism (i.e., refusal to recognize the gods revered in the official cults) on the other. Some Christian teachers, notably Noetus, Praxeas and Sabellius, argued that the distinctions "within" the godhead called "father," "son," and "spirit" described successions of modes or operations of the divine unity. See E. Evans, introduction to *Tertullian, Adversus Praxean* (London: Routledge, 1948), pp. 6-31.

do. In the same way: the supreme God would not be supreme unless he ruled over other gods. Only this sort of power would do justice to the greatness of God and redound to his honor.[64]

[Matt. 22.29–30; Exod. 31.18]
You say, "The immortal angels stand before God, those who are not subject to human passion, and these we speak of as gods because they are near the godhead." Why do we argue about names? Is this [difference of opinion] not really a difference over names? The one whom the Greeks call Athena is called Minerva by the Romans, and she is called other things by the Egyptians, the Syrians, the Thracians, and so on. Is something lost (I think not!) in addressing the goddess by different names?

　　Whether one addresses these divine beings as gods or angels matters very little, since their nature remains the same. Matthew supports this when he writes, "Jesus answered and

---

64. That is to say, those who are godlike in being and nature, a class of immortals like that comprising the Roman pantheon. The philosopher employs the familiar argument that there is as much distance between the gods and men as between men and animals. Hence God is monarchial only if one imagines an order of divine beings over which he has supreme authority—as an earthly king would over his subjects. On the diversity of the created order, cf. Plotinus, 6 *Ennead* 7.14–16.

Macarius is at his strongest in response to this objection, accusing his opponent of reasoning from nominal or generic similarity to actual likeness: "God alone is god absolutely. . . . [He rules] not by virtue of having the same name as other gods and hence alongside of them, but as supreme and without being one of them." The creator God of Christian thought, unlike the supreme god of Hellenistic speculation, derives his right to rule over creation by virtue of a divine prerogative. Porphyry's critique implies the view that the God of Christian teaching rules over natures essentially *unlike* his own and hence violates the order of nature, which he is thought to have established. A man may claim to be king over creatures like himself, but king only in a figurative way over creatures unlike himself (i.e., lord or master). The analogy employed is that of a king and his subjects versus a shepherd and his flocks. Macarius seems not to worry over this point; he claims that God's rule is necessarily a rule over the inferior because the divine being has no equal.

said, 'You do err, for you know neither the scriptures nor the power of God, for in the resurrection, they do not marry nor are they given in marriage but are like the angels in heaven.' " Is this not a confession that [angels] have a share in the divine nature? [And those] who make images as objects of veneration for the gods do not imagine that God [himself] is in the wood or the stone or the bronze used in the making of the image.

They do not think for a moment that if a part of the image is cut off that the power of God is thereby lessened. Such images—such as those of animals and those in temples—were erected by ancient peoples for the sake of evoking the memory of the god. They were created so that those who saw them would remember the god or would take time out to perform ritual cleansings, or to make easier the act of prayer, whereby each person supplicates the god for the particular things of which he has need.

I hasten to add that if one makes an image of a friend he does not confuse the icon with the friend or believe that the parts of his friend's body are incorporated into the representation. Just so, in the case of sacrifices offered to the gods: the [sacrifices] are not so much an honor paid to the gods as evidence that the worshipers are grateful for what they have received. Furthermore, it seems fitting that the forms of these statues are generally the form of a man because man is the noblest of creatures and an image of God.

The Christians seem to endorse this when they conceive of God as having fingers which he sometimes uses in order to write, as when it is said, "He gave the two tables to Moses, which were written by the finger of God." And the Christians [too], imitating our ways, erect temples and build great houses in which they assemble for prayer, even though they are enjoined to do this in their own houses—since the Lord can hear them wherever they are.[65]

---

65. Crafer's translation of this passage has led him to conclude that the erection of great houses or churches implies a time for the writing after 312, "before which date the archaeological evidence for distinctively Christian places of worship is scant." This opinion, however, is susceptible to revision in the light of Christian archaeological evidence from the past fifty years,

Even if someone among the Greeks were silly enough to
think that gods dwelled in statues,[66] his idea would be more

---

which suggests that churches had become vast charitable institutions, with
buildings and estates to match their growing responsibilities. The data are
surveyed comprehensively in the Acts of the IX. International Congress of
Christian Archaeology (*ACIAC*: Rome: Pontifical Inst. of Christian
Archaeology, 1978); and see W. H. C. Frend, "Church and People in the Third
Century," in his survey, *The Rise of Christianity* (Philadelphia: Fortress,
1984), pp. 398-425.

The philosopher's comments make good sense if written before the edicts
of toleration in the early fourth century: specifically, the Christians refused
to acknowledge the legal impediments to the practice of their faith, and
built shrines to rival those of their pagan opponents. A date toward the
end of the third century would seem the most plausible. When in February
303 the emperor Diocletian turned his attention to the Christian upper classes,
or *honestiores*, in Roman society, he ordered the attacks be made on the
organization of the church rather than on ordinary believers; hence, church
buildings and the "possessions" of the churches—books of scripture and
sacred vessels used in celebration—were targeted. Pagan critics of the
period—including Porphyry—made it clear that the Christians were guilty
of accepting "Jewish myths" at face value and had made a criminal into
the hero of their cult. See the comments of Lactantius (who was an eyewitness
of the events of 303) in his *Institutes* 5.2 and those of Eusebius, *Preparation
for the Gospel* 1.2.

The philosopher's point concerning the "physical" nature of God has
suffered mutation. If the objection is held to be apposite to Macarius' response,
then it should argue that while the use of images was advocated by the
ancients in order to encourage piety, representations of the supreme God
are impious. In view of the uncertainty over the identity of Macarius, it
is difficult to assess how well developed the Christian iconography of his
day may have been. Porphyry seems to have objected only to literary imagery,
suggesting contradictions in Christian interpretation of Jewish scripture; cf.
Hoffmann, *Celsus*, pp. 114-119, and Plotinus, 5 *Ennead* 3.15f.

66. In his response Macarius follows the line that the blessedness of
the Christian heaven consists in the absence of death and decay, hence in
the exclusion of "physical union" in preference for "rational existence
. . . associated with the world of immortality." The worldly corollary of this
rational existence is taken to be avoidance of marriage and the "symbols
of corruption," marriage being considered a symbol of irrational, sensate
(sexual) existence. Patristic commendations of the unmarried life can be
traced conceptually to Paul and to early eastern monastic practice. While

sensible than that of the man who believes that the Divine Being entered into the womb of the virginal Mary to become her unborn son—and then was born, swaddled, [hauled off] to the place of blood and gall, and all the rest of it.[67]

---

the Council of Elvira in 306 endorsed celibacy for bishops, the Council of Nicaea in 325 rejected a proposal to compel clergy of all ranks to give up cohabitation with their wives. The issue was, in any case, at the forefront of discussion in the fourth-century church.

Macarius' circuitous reply is an attempt to say that there is no fundamental disagreement between the teaching of the gospel and "true philosophy" over the value of sexual abstinence. Porphyry's point, however, is that Christians in fact recognize a multiplicity of divine powers in acknowledging that the angels—whom he equates with the gods—have a share in the divine nature, and that the expression of these powers in human form as icons is not unreasonable if man is held to be made in God's image. He uses Matt. 22.29-30 to document the inconsistency of Christian teaching in the matter of worship and icon veneration.

67. Macarius' interesting use of the Helios metaphor, which also plays a role in defining the Nicene and post-Nicene formulation of the divine sonship of Christ, is not entirely relevant to the philosopher's simple comparison of two kinds of belief: It is far less absurd to think that God lives in statues than to believe that the divine being implanted itself in a virgin, and in the course of time was born, lived, and died as a human being. Macarius' reply shows little awareness of the mid-fifth-century Chalcedonian orthodoxy concerning the "two natures" of Christ, and indeed departs in certain respects from the emergent trinitarian orthodoxy of the fourth century: thus, "The word is made flesh, but does not lower itself to the disease [death?] or humiliation of the flesh. . . . For just as the sun when it descends into the wetness [of the sea] does not get wet . . . so, too, God the Word . . . while descending to the flesh [assumes nothing corrupt from it]." The orthodox had long used the sun as a means of describing the unique generation of the son from the father: the rays of the sun are "perpetually" generated by the sun; nevertheless, they are not divisible from its essence nor inferior to it. Macarius seems to confuse the application of the image in saying that the *logos* was as "unaffected" by human nature as is the sun in its daily descent into the sea. More to the point is his assertion that God is reckoned to have used mud (Gen. 2.7) in creating mankind and hence found it reasonable to "wear flesh from a virgin . . . taking the mixture which is more precious than clay, and making from it an image stamped with his godhead."

[Exod 22.28]

Might I also show you a passage where that awful word "gods" crops up, this time from the Law of Moses, where the book veritably shouts to the reader, "You shall not revile gods; you shall not curse a ruler of your people." The passage has clear reference to gods who are already familiar to us—for example, those envisaged in the words "You shall not chase after other gods" [Jer. 7.6]; and "If you go and worship other gods . . ." [Deut. 11.28].[68]

These are gods and not men who are considered worthy of reverence by us. Both Moses and his successor Joshua speak clearly of these gods—as when Joshua says to the people, "Fear him, serve him only and put away the gods your fathers served" [Josh. 24.14]. It is not about men but about the gods that Paul writes when he says of the spiritual principles, "Though there be so-called gods, whether on earth or in heaven, still to us there is but one God and father, from whom are all things" [1 Cor. 8.5].

You are mistaken to think that [the supreme] God is angry if anyone other than himself is called a god. Indeed, rulers do not refuse the title from their subjects; masters [receive the title] from their slaves. Is it right to think that God is more petulant in this regard than men?[69]

---

68. Wrongly cited by Crafer as Deut. 12.28.

69. The philosopher's point is that neither Christianity nor Judaism is consistent in the matter of monotheistic outlook. The biblical tradition, with its acknowledgment of the gods of other tribes and nations, stands in tension with the formulations of Christian teachers from Justin Martyr onward, who juxtapose a "settled" biblical monotheism derived from Judaism with the glimmers of monotheistic thought derived from philosophy. See Justin's discussion, 1 *Apology* 59.

From the pagan perspective the Christian position appears more inconsistent by virtue of two doctrines: the doctrine of angels, which passed in a developed form from apocalyptic Judaism into first century Christianity, and the belief in the coequal divinity of father, son and spirit within an indivisible godhead. The Christian habit of denying the title "god" to any power other than the fully articulated trinity of persons seems incoherent to the philosopher.

Macarius, on the other hand, argues that the things called "gods" in scripture are not gods at all and have no independent existence; rather, they are mistakes made by the ancients in their attempts to intellectualize the divine realm. Porphyry seems to anticipate this defense in his suggestion that different ranks of divine beings are mentioned in scripture without any indication that they are illusory (cf. Gen. 1.26; 6.2; 6.4, etc.).

11

Critique of the Resurrection of the Flesh

Apocrit. IV.24

Returning to consider again the matter of the resurrection of the dead: For what purpose should God intervene in this way, completely and arbitrarily overturning a course of events that has always been held good—namely, the plan, ordained by him at the beginning, through which whole races are preserved and do not come to an end.

The natural law established and approved by God, lasting through the ages, is by its very nature unchanging and thus not to be overturned by [the God] who fashioned it. Nor is it to be demolished as though it were a body of laws invented by a mere mortal to serve his own limited purposes. It is preposterous to think that when the whole [race] is destroyed there follows a resurrection; that [God] raises with a wave of his hand a man who died three years before the resurrection [of Jesus] and those like Priam and Nestor who lived a thousand years before, together with those who lived when the human race was new.

Just to think of this silly teaching makes me light-headed. Many have perished at sea; their bodies have been eaten by scavenging fish. Hunters have been eaten by their prey, the wild animals, and birds. How will their bodies rise up?

Or let us take an example to test this little doctrine, so innocently put forward [by the Christians]: A certain man was shipwrecked. The hungry fish had his body for a feast. But the fish were caught and cooked and eaten by some fishermen, who had the misfortune to run afoul of some ravenous dogs, who killed and ate them. When the dogs died, the vultures came and made a feast of them.

How will the body of the shipwrecked man be reassembled, considering it has been absorbed by other bodies of various kinds? Or take a body that has been consumed by fire or a body that has been food for the worms: how can these bodies be restored to the essence of what they were originally?

Ah! You say: "All things are possible with God." But this is not true. Not all things are possible for him. [God] cannot make it happen that Homer should not have been a poet. God cannot bring it about that Troy should not fall. He cannot make $2 \times 2 = 100$ rather than 4, even though he should prefer it to be so. He cannot become evil, even if he wished to. Being good by nature, he cannot sin. And it is no weakness on his part that he is unable to do these things—to sin or to become evil.

[Mortals] on the other hand may have an inclination and even an ability for doing a certain thing; if something interferes to keep them from doing it, it's clear that it is their weakness that's to blame. [I repeat]: God to be god is by nature good: he is not prevented from being evil. It is simply not in the divine nature to be bad.

There is a final point: How terrible it would be if God the Creator should stand helplessly by and see the heavens melting away in a storm of fire—the stars falling, the earth dying. For no one has ever imagined anything more glorious than the beauty of the heavens.

Yet you say, "He will raise up the rotten and stinking corpses of men," some of them, no doubt, belonging to worthy men, but others having no grace or merit prior to death. A very unpleasant sight it will be. And even if God should refashion the dead bodies, making them more tolerable than before, there is still this: it would be impossible for the earth to accommodate all those who have died from the beginning of the world if they should be raised from the dead.[70]

---

70. This critique of the resurrection of the dead (flesh) derives from the belief that only mind and spirit can know God—hence the reconstitution of the decomposed flesh would serve no purpose. In the Platonic scheme the body is the chief hindrance of the soul in search of God, as Christian teachers from Athenagoras (2nd cent.) onward were aware. In his treatise "On the Resurrection of the Dead," Athenagoras makes the points (a) that resurrection is not impossible; (b) that the God who created the world can raise the dead; (c) that the resurrected body is different from the physical body; and (d) that the judgment of the world "requires" humanity to stand before God in bodily form, since accountability for actions, good and bad, must have reference to the agent through which they were performed. In dealing with certain objections to the doctrine already current in the second century, Athenagoras launches (*Apology* IV) into a discussion of the processes of digestion which prevent the victims of plague, shipwreck and war "who have become the food of animals [and are deprived of burial]" from undergoing the natural process of decomposition. His discussion leads him to conclude that the ingestion and digestion of human flesh by animals is a "refining" process whereby whatever is harmful, useless and hurtful to the nature of the animal (i.e., whatever is essentially human) is expelled through excretion or vomiting. Athenagoras does not seem to perceive that his lengthy description contradicts his premiss that the resurrected body is fundamentally different from the one susceptible of decay.

Celsus had charged that the Christians misunderstood Plato's theory of reincarnation, "and believe the absurd notion that the corporeal body will be raised and reconstituted by God, and that somehow they will actually see God with their mortal eyes and hear him with their ears and be able to touch him with their hands" (Hoffmann, *Celsus*, p. 110). Early apologists, such as Justin Martyr in the second century, had based their defense of the resurrection almost exclusively on scriptural passages; cf. 1 *Apology* 19.

The Christian position was dichotomous: to the extent that a good God had created humankind and had undertaken to redeem it, the body was "equipped" for salvation as a temple of the spirit. The ideals of self-denial, sexual abstinence and celibacy, and the more basic question of what sort of body could be raised given the role of the body in the perdurance of human sinfulness, combined to produce various ingenious answers to pagan commonsensical objections to the doctrine of bodily resurrection. A fifth-century Christian teacher assured a friend stricken with arthritis that at the resurrection God "would make our nature translucent . . . [human flesh will] turn molten to regain its solidity," as a base metal turned gold in an alchemist's crucible.

On the subject of Christian ambivalence toward the body in general, see Peter Brown's excellent discussion, *The Body and Society: Men, Women and Sexual Renunciation in Early Christianity* (New York: Columbia Univ. Press, 1988), here citing p. 441.

Epilogue

From Babylon to Rome: The Contexts of Jewish-Christian-Pagan Interaction through Porphyry

For its first three centuries, Christianity thrived as a religion of the persecuted. Jesus of Nazareth—an itinerant preacher who became a disciple of John the Baptist just prior to the latter's arrest for treason—had died as a Jewish victim of Roman administrative insecurity in a land always held in contempt by its neighbors and viewed with suspicion by its Roman governors. From the Roman standpoint he was one of hundreds of suspected Jewish "bandits" who suffered the exemplary death of crucifixion—a public warning to the Jews that the protection granted to the practice of their religion was an act of largess which could be withdrawn or curtailed at any time.

The life-story of Jesus of Nazareth and the early church belongs to the history of anti-Jewish feeling in general and Roman anti-Judaism in particular. Judaism simultaneously intrigued and frustrated the Romans. It intrigued them because of its claim to represent religious traditions older than those of the Greeks and Persians, whose gods and observances had been imported piecemeal over the three centuries preceding the common era. It infuriated them because—unlike the

95

religions of other ancient cultures—it had developed (in its orthodox form at any rate) an exclusive attachment to one god—Yahweh—which left no room for a casual approach to divine arithmetic. Yahweh was to be worshiped with one's whole heart, soul and mind, to the exclusion of all other powers in heaven or on the earth. This belief, however, was not based on philosophical premises, and for this reason the term "monotheism" fails to express the nature of Israel's faith.

THE GOD CONCEPT AND ITS POLITICAL CONSEQUENCES

The God concept with which Israel began was basically polytheistic (Exod. 20.3). God was limited in power (Exod. 4.24) and local in character (Exod. 18.5; 33.3; 14–16). The most that could be claimed for Yahweh was that as a national god he protected his people from neighboring peoples and their gods. His throne was on the high mountain; storm and volcanic phenomena were taken as manifestations of his presence (Exod. 19.16–19; 33.9f.; 40.34–38).

The transition from desert to settled life on the land (believed to be his gift to a "chosen" people) produced a change in the character of this God paralleling the change in the people's fortunes. Yahweh became the god of the armies of Israel, a war God—the God of hosts—who aided Israel in the subjugation of neighboring peoples or the defense of territory already taken. His other face, if not benevolent, was less severe: as giver of land, he was also the *baal* (fertilizer) of the soil and took responsibility for its fertility and for the rain, as well as for the famines that were occasionally used to winnow the population and the floods that might be sent to wash away the unrighteous, "as in the time of Noah" (Gen. 6.1f.).

As revealed in his political dealings with his chosen people, Yahweh was fickle. Peace and security are less thematic in the history of Israel than political instability, warfare and religious apostasy. Around 930 B.C.E Israel fell into political and religious pieces and in 721, the northern kingdom of Israel was overrun by the Assyrians. The comparatively weak tribe of Judah to the south carried the cult of Yahweh forward into the sixth century, but by 586 B.C.E. it had lost it political and religious identity. The warnings and wailing of the prophets, who began during this time to insist on God's interest in procuring justice and his moral character as "having no favorites," their assertion that divine approval could not be secured by sacrifices, offerings, and "bribes" is interesting in terms of the history of theology. From the standpoint of political history, however, the prophets are a distraction. They warned the little nation that its time was up, and up it was.

While it is obviously impossible to say *when* the inhabitants of Judah became "monotheistic," the political outcome of the kingdom's involvement with Babylon had the effect of discrediting the earlier God concepts. Although Yahweh never loses his military bearing—as the later history of apocalyptic Judaism and the messiah faiths illustrate—his ability to command armies, or for that matter the loyalty of his followers, is submerged beneath the new thinking that God invites, pleads, warns, chastises; above all, he can be offended—hurt—in his efforts to deal fairly with his own, to whom he prefers to show mercy.

Read back into the history of Yahweh, the new God concept suggested that the nation of Judah (Israel earlier) had fallen not because of a failure of the chosen people-*ideal* but as a penalty for disregarding the demands of an *ethical* God, one who invites obedience to his law because it is fundamentally good, right and just and who hates and spurns the pilgrim feasts and burnt sacrifices offered to him under the *ancien régime*. Monotheism, or, more precisely, the belief that Yahweh alone is God in the sense of having exclusive title to the name, arises from the ashes of the earlier God concept, according to which Yahweh was supposed to guarantee the political survival of the nation. That concept, self-evidently, had failed. "Second"-Isaiah (Isa. 42.18-22) pictured Israel as a deaf and blind pawn of rulers and tyrants who suffered, as slaves suffer, without hope of reward or rest (Isa. 53.7-8). The new belief in an ethical god had the effect of explaining political fortune as being due not to God's arbitrary exercise of power, but to his chosen people's failure to recognize his true character. It was they who had failed, not their god.

THE POLITICAL DIMENSION

This belief came at a political price. The many-godded nations of the ancient world, ranging from Babylon to Syria to Rome, found Jewish exclusivism a sticking point in their attempts to establish political rule over the kingdoms of Israel and Judah. When political solutions and religious toleration wore thin, as with the Babylonians in 587, military options and direct rule were tried. While none succeeded entirely in wiping away the Yahwist cult, which centered on Jerusalem after the sixth century B.C.E., the physical size of the Jewish kingdoms shrank from an area extending from Ezion Geber in the south to Riblah in the north (a distance of about 350 miles and about 120 miles at its widest point) in the tenth century B.C.E. to an area of about 110 by 60 miles, extending from Galilee in the north to Masada in the south under the Roman procurators (ca. 54 C.E.). Between Judah's capitulation to Babylon and the deportation ("exile") in the sixth century and the burning of the Temple in Jerusalem by the Romans in 70 C.E. there were periods of remission and relative calm. The period of Persian domination, beginning with the Persian king Cyrus's conquest of Babylon in 539, is remembered as one such period. Cyrus encouraged the spread of Aramaic—the language later spoken by the inhabitants of northern Judea around Galilee (and presumably also by Jesus) and ordered the rebuilding of the temple in Jerusalem, which had been gutted by the Babylonians.

Those Jews who returned from exile to live under Persian "protection" in Jerusalem were a changed people. Grim experience had taught them that their religious customs were not well liked. The response to the Assyrian and Babylonian "conquests" of Palestine was retrenchment—a hunkering down behind newly built city walls designed to keep the strangers out and the faith locked in. With Ezra and Nehemiah, whoever they may have been, and whose story is not recovered until the fourth century before Jesus, the face of Judaism changed: Whatever expansionist ambitions may still have defined the religious quest to make Yahweh king of kings, lord of lords, they were replaced in the fifth century by the more practical aim of survival and preservation of a faith under siege by its neighbors.

THE LAW

A cliché of the period is that the Jews "built a hedge around the Law" for its protection and their own. According to a tradition (which today is regarded as a simplification of a long historical process) the Jews who stayed on in Mesopotamia rather than return to Jerusalem favored a consolidation of Judaism in Jerusalem. This "consolidation" was reflected in three events: the rebuilding of the temple—a slow, slipshod and arduous process—the rebuilding of the walls around the city of Jerusalem, and the promulgation of the law of Moses as the law of the Jewish people and of the city of Jerusalem in particular. The extent, originality and antiquity of this "Mosaic law" is hard to determine since in its biblical form it is transparently a mixture of Babylonian law, tribal custom and (priestly) purification rules. Even a much later critic of Judaism and Christianity such as Porphyry thinks that the law of Moses was somehow mysteriously lost and "reinvented" in the time of Ezra.

What is clear even from the self-interested biblical sources is that the "application" and observance of the law prior to the Babylonian conquest were repeatedly thwarted by religiously ambivalent figures like Mannaseh and Amon, who had a custom of satisfying an apparently unquenchable religious appetite for altars and sacrificial poles devoted to the baals and their female companions, the asherahs (2 Chron. 33). Prior to the conquest, Judah was in a polytheistic spiral.

The ruler credited by tradition with turning things around is Josiah, supposedly eight years old when he came to the throne to rule Jerusalem for thirty-one years. Josiah is represented by the biblical writers and editors as the best king since David: At the age of twenty, he is reputed to have given the order to purge Jerusalem of the shrines, altars and poles devoted to "foreign" gods—chiefly those of the Babylonians. With typical Middle Eastern hyperbole, he is depicted as ordering the altars destroyed in his presence, making dust of the molten images of the gods, then "strewing it over the graves of those who sacrificed to them" (2 Chron. 34.4). Faithful to the God of his fathers as he may have been, he seems to have extorted money for the rebuilding of the temple as a punitive tax on the Jews who had flirted with the worship of the baals—especially the inhabitants of the northern reaches of the country, who were forever being accused of being soft on idolatry by their more orthodox southern cousins. The violations of Yahweh's cult are understood by the priestly writers, from their purview in Jerusalem, as grassroots rural or populist movements which needed periodically to be brought under control by those technically responsible for safeguarding ancient traditions. The Maccabean movement of the second century B.C.E., originally centered on the rural "shrines" of Lydda and Modein, the Essene and Baptist movements which may have sprung up shortly thereafter, suggest that the official view of Palestinian rural religion is not entirely accurate. The Yahwism of the Maccabeans declined steadily in relation to the Hellenized Yahwist movement in Jerusalem. Within Palestine generally, the rural areas were selectively and unpredictably more "conservative" and less observant of the law.

In two places the Hebrew bible recounts the legend of the "discovery" of the law of Moses under Josiah: 2 Kings 22.8–10, copied by the author of 2 Chron. 34. The story has all the earmarks of a legend designed to conceal more mundane origins for the books of Moses. In fact, Judah had been only slightly more hostile to the worship of foreign gods than the northern kingdom of Israel. The centralization of the cult of Yahweh in Jerusalem, coupled with the tale of Josiah's razing of the altars, and the discovery of the law are designed to enforce the view that just prior to the catastrophe of exile the religion of Judah was its old self, for one brief, shining and atypical moment.

According to the biblical legend, the high priest Hilkiah finds "the book of the law of the Lord given by Moses" on a routine inspection of the building site. He presents it to a certain Shaphan, the king's secretary, who dutifully reads it to the king. In a gesture designed to show his anguish, Josiah rends his clothes upon hearing the words spoken for the first time, "because our fathers have not kept the word of the law [nor done what] is written in this book" (2 Chron. 34.21).

Like all legends, this story seems to have an historical

core. But equally like all legends, the core is not the whole story. What would later be recognized as "orthodox" Jewish observance would have been as strange in the context of the mixed religious cults of sixth-century Jerusalem as the Judaism of the Ethiopian Falashas appeared in the twentieth. The scene of all the inhabitants of Jerusalem—"both great and small"— standing before Josiah at a massive Passover celebration to swear their loyalty to a scroll squirreled away by his forefathers is legendary, as is the tale of Josiah's cleanup operation. Yet beneath the legend lurks a fact or two concerning the lapse into ancient elohimist practices and the slovenly state of the temple cult. The ban on the worship of "foreign" gods and goddesses under Josiah serves a dramatic purpose. It is an episode required if the "tragedy" of the Babylonian conquest and deportation is to mean anything at all.

The interlude of "good king Josiah" is followed by the eleven-year reign of his sons, one of whom, Jehoiakim, was taken in fetters to Babylon along with a sizable number of the sacred vessels of the temple. Apparently his fate was considered just deserts for "the abominations which he did and what was found against him"—capitulation to the king of Babylon, Nebuchadnezzar. Jehoiakim's sons are remembered chiefly for being even worse than their father—in particular Zedekiah, "who did not humble himself before Jeremiah the prophet" and dragged the leading priests and people with him into apostasy.

The myth of a "faithful" Zion, a remnant of the patriarchal faith resistant to the idolatry of Babylon, Egypt, and Persia, grew out of the nostalgia for a golden age and the hope for its return. The latter would finally express itself in the messianic faith of the Roman period. Abraham, Moses, and David were the pillars of this memory, not Jeroboam, Ahab and Zedekiah who had driven the kingdoms into apostasy and who, according to the rabbis of Jesus' day, "would have no part in the kingdom of God" when it came.

After the fall of Babylon and following the exile this nostalgia was encouraged by the Persian king Cyrus. It was not the returnees who agitated to rebuild the city walls and the ruined temple of Yahweh, but Cyrus, the foreigner, the

worshiper of other gods. Thus, the chronicler of this period
of Jewish history reports Cyrus as saying, following the victory
of the Persians over the Babylonians:

> The Lord, the God of heaven has given me all the kingdoms
> of the earth and has charged me to build him a house at
> Jerusalem, which is in Judah. Whoever is among you of all
> his people, may the Lord his God be with him.

So dependent was the Judaism of the sixth century and
later on the initiatives of Cyrus and his successors that he
is made an honorary Jew, a *mashia* (deliverer), a member of
the Yahwist cult. It was the foreigner who ordered the temple
rebuilt, the stranger who ordered that the law of Moses be
proclaimed as the law of the region. He had done for the Jews
what they could not do—politically or religiously—for
themselves. He restored their cult, their temple, their city and
their law to them.

Theological analysis of the religious situation during the
time of the captivity seems to have flourished chiefly among
the "leading men" in exile, probably those whose theological
view of history persuaded them that their punishment had
something to do with forsaking ancestral customs—especially
the keeping of a "national" Passover. It is doubtful that the
Jews who were deported to Babylon were "monotheistic" in
any speculative sense. They were men who tended to interpret
historical events and political outcomes theologically by raising
questions about the will, purposes and justice of God. In their
collective view, bad times were the consequence of bad actions,
of "sin" or a loss of national purity. Isaiah, Micah, and Jeremiah
were interpreted to have foreseen the apostasy of the nation
and its punishment as part of a divine plan. If the battle was
lost, it was because Yahweh wished to chastise them (and
so joined the opposing forces to fight with his brother gods
against his own people); if famine came, it was because Yahweh
had been cheated of his share of the harvest; and if exile came,
it was because Yahweh had permitted the strange gods
worshiped by his enemies to get the political upper hand. The
romanticized summary of this, often attributed to the time of

Josiah (ca. 621 B.C.E.), with its repetition of the law and ritual blessings and curses, was read back to the time of Moses, as a form of vitiated Yahwist orthodoxy, though in large measure it represents a much later reaction to the nation's apostasy and to the exile itself (cf. Deut. 27.15 and 29–30).

The exclusive worship of Yahweh, enshrined in the law, is advocated as a religious solution to the problem of political misfortune. Still burned deeply in the Jewish psyche of Jesus' day however, is the ancient vignette of Exod. 32.7, when the newly delivered children of Yahweh dance and prostrate themselves before a golden bull-calf—the symbol of the Canaanite cults out of which Yahwism had emerged. Far from being purged or forgotten, it was preserved in the structure of the horned altar, such as the one at Megiddo, the sacrifice of bulls and the erection of sacred poles (Exod. 24.4ff.). Equally vivid was Jeremiah's description of Judah's religion before the fall: "You, Judah, have as many gods as you have towns; you have set up as many altars to burn sacrifices to baal as there are streets in Jerusalem. Offer up no prayer for these people; raise no cry or prayer on their behalf, for I will not listen when they call to me in their hour of disaster" (Jer. 11.13–14).

It was in the interest of the foreign overlords of Judah to promote and guarantee Jewish religious identity in exchange for Jewish political obedience. It took a royal decree to install the "law" of Moses as the law of Jerusalem and Judah, and it took Cyrus and his successor Darius to make it happen.

According to tradition, Ezra and Nehemiah had urged the "restored" Jerusalem community not to enter into any foreign alliances. In practical terms, the community held itself aloof from the mixed cult in Samaria in the north of Palestine. Samaria was seen as the "worst case" of religious mixing. Following the conquest of the region by the Assyrians, foreign settlers had moved into the land and married into the local population. Their descendants appear to have worshiped Yahweh as a fertility God (2 Kings 17), but the Jerusalem community did not recognize the Samaritans as Israelites and hostility—leading finally in 128 B.C.E. to outright warfare—existed between the two branches of the Yahwist cult from the fourth century onward. Ironically, the bond that might have held Jew and Samaritan together after the withdrawal of the Samaritan Yahwists to their temple on Mount Gerizim—namely the Law of Moses—did nothing to heal the ancestral wound. From the standpoint of the isolationist Judaeans, the Samaritans were lukewarm Yahwists at best and idolaters at worst. Jewish pilgrims *en route* to Jerusalem for festivals through Samaritan territory expected rough treatment (Luke 9.51-56) and usually got it. In Christian history, the Samaritans are remembered flatteringly as having accepted the gospel more readily than the Judaeans (Acts 8.4-25), and after some initial hesitation about launching the messianic preaching in the north of Palestine (Matt. 10.5-6), the region became fertile ground for converts to Christianity.

HELLENISM

In 333 B.C.E. at the battle of Issus, Alexander the Great defeated the Persian king Darius III. The Persian era, during which an articulated Jewish identity was established, came to an end. Alexander's goal was to open up a route by way of Syria and Palestine to Egypt. The effect on the Jews in Palestine was direct and immediate. The Jews submitted peaceably to Greek rule, and in recognition of their good sense they were permitted to continue practicing their cult without interference. Their legal status was unchanged, but nothing would remain the same.

Palestine swarmed with Greek traders, merchants, and travelers. Admiration of Greek manners, architecture, habits of thought, and literature was encouraged, and throughout the Near East ancestral languages were traded for the language of Sophocles and Plato or approximations of it. Greek settlements were founded; Tyre was repopulated with Greeks and Samaria with Macedonians (a penalty for having resisted the Greek advance into northern Palestine). Outside Jerusalem, Greek civil law was imposed and within Judaea Greek was introduced as the language of trade. Minor officials in Jerusalem, in their later dealings with Roman occupation forces, communicated in Greek not Latin, and Greek (not Aramaic or Hebrew) was the language in which the sayings of Jesus and later the missionary propaganda of the church—the gospels—were circulated. It has even been suggested with some plausibility, but no relevance, that Jesus knew a little Greek. Paul (or his secretaries, since he seems to have been illiterate: 1 Cor. 16.21) used only Greek in his letters to the newly formed Christian churches of the Graeco-Roman world.

With their language Greek colonists brought their own patterns of life, their own customs: Greek buildings, baths, gymnasiums, amphitheaters, rhetorical skills, and medical practice. The custom of debate and "didactic conversation" in pursuit of the truth—the question-and-answer method now usually associated with rabbinical Judaism—was a feature of Greek, not Near Eastern culture. The habit of reclining (i.e., resting on the left elbow while using the right hand for eating) for festival meals was also widely adopted. It was the customary "position" at mealtime by Jesus' day.

As a people who mistrusted the ways of the stranger but had become accustomed to his presence, the more cosmopolitan Jews of Jerusalem adapted quickly to Greek culture. By the second century B.C.E., there were Jews who earnestly believed that they were the kinsmen of the Spartans, and who equated the proverbial fairness of Spartan law with the law of Moses. In 1 Macc. 12.21 there is a description of a letter from Arius, king of Sparta, to Onias I, the high priest in Jerusalem (ca. 300 B.C.E.); the letter "reveals" that an ancient document has been discovered which identifies the Spartans and Jews as brothers, both descended from the tribe of Abraham. And while the Jews in Jerusalem flirted guiltily with Hellenistic civilization, the Philistines and Phoenicians surrendered themselves less cautiously to the Greek way of life.

Gymnasia were built where the youth of the city (priests among them) romped about—in Greek fashion—unclothed. Ridiculed for the "mark" of their circumcision by Greek spectators at these games, masses of the young men of Jerusalem underwent an improvised piece of surgery to create a new penile foreskin to disguise their identity (1 Macc. 1.15), an operation still performed in Jesus' day and among the Jews of the diaspora in the first century C.E. (1 Cor. 7.18).

In 175 B.C.E. the high priest in Jerusalem was Onias III. By this time, Jerusalem had fallen under Syrian control, following the death of Alexander in 323 B.C.E. and a period of rule by the Hellenized Ptolemies of Egypt. The Jerusalem community had experienced a century and a half of Greek culture by this point. More aggressive in their pursuit of "political Hellenization"—the belief that the enforcement of Greek ways and styles would make for a stable empire (*oikoumenē*, indicating Greek as opposed to barbarian culture)—the Syrian protectors of Palestine manipulated the high priesthood, the main stay of Jewish orthodoxy. Onias is remembered as a devout observer of the Mosaic law. His brother Joshua, on the other hand, was a leader of a band of "renegade Jews" (1 Macc. 1.11) who wished to enter into a treaty with the gentiles "because disaster upon disaster has overtaken us since we segregated ourselves from them." After striking a deal with the Syrians to have his brother ousted and himself installed as high priest, Joshua changed his name to Jason and arranged for Onias' murder in Antioch. In 160, the deposed priest's son established a "temple" in the Egyptian city of Leontopolis modeled on the Jerusalem temple, under the protection of the Egyptian court. In Jerusalem, Jason sped along the process of integration.

After three years, another Hellenized priest, a certain Menelaus, offered the Syrian king a higher sum than Jason had offered for the high priesthood. Accordingly Jason was deposed and Menelaus installed. Jason then raised armed troops to recover the priesthood, which he did successfully in 170, with the intervention of the Syrian king Antiochus. Menelaus was restored and assumed the title "ruler" of Jerusalem. But the Syrians were firmly in control. The temple treasury was plundered as Menelaus tried to keep pace with increasing demands for the "protection" money desperately needed by the Syrians to fight their wars against Egypt. Impatient with the Jewish leadership, Antiochus decided in 169 to plunder the temple treasury outright to replenish his own; in the process he looted the temple, taking the seven-branched lampstand, and the altar of incense to Antioch (1 Macc. 1.20–24).

In the next two years a series of measures were taken

to ensure the completion of the "Hellenization" of the Jewish homeland. The walls of Jerusalem were (again) torn down and a fortress was built on mount Zion; Jews were forbidden to keep the sabbath or to circumcize their children. Although pious memory has recorded these measures as "outrages," it is certain that many Jews of Jerusalem were sympathetic to this "final solution." The wealthy and the intelligentsia were tired of isolation from the good things the Greek world had to offer, not least prosperity and learning. Circumcision was already out of vogue among certain classes, especially the youth of the city, and the citified priests had often encouraged the identification of Yahweh with the Greek *Theos Hypsistos*— the high God, equivalent to Zeus in the Greek pantheon. The erection of an altar to Zeus in place of the altar of burnt offering in 167 and the introduction of pigs as sacrificial animals were designed to make the equivalence of Zeus and Yahweh explicit. From the Greek point of view, religion had to do fundamentally with the worship of the "true" God. What one called him— Zeus, Yahweh, El or Baal—was a matter of no great importance.

The books of the Maccabees, the primary documentation for this cloudy period of Jewish history, are written (ca. 124–100 B.C.E.) from the standpoint of those opposed to the religious innovations of the Syrian period in the rule of Palestine. Passionately written though they are, it is clear from what they say (and from what is not said) that Jerusalem was on the brink and that Judaism was dying, not through military action but through assimilation.

When opposition came, it came from beyond the rubble of the city walls, primarily as a reaction to Syrian political meddling but also as a response to the destruction of the temple cult. Syrian inspectors roamed the countryside ostensibly to enforce compliance with the new regulations concerning pagan sacrifice and also to facilitate setting up rural shrines. One clan in Modein, the Hasmoneans, led by their patriarch Mattathias, refused to comply and took to the hills where they formed a renegade army determined to fight a war of attrition against Syrian interference in the cult. Judas, the son of Mattathias, assumed leadership after his father's death and soon earned the name *makkaba* (hammer) for the band's devastating small-scale guerrilla attacks, many of them directed at apostate Jews rather than against the Syrians.

There is no evidence that the hellenized Jews of Jerusalem wanted saving from their apostasy, though the Book of Daniel, composed around the time of the Syrian occupation, seems to represent the view of some Jews that the end of history and the judgment of God would follow the desecration of the temple cult—an apocalyptic vision of the world that remained popular well into the Christian era.

Whether the "renegade Jews" of Jerusalem wanted saving or not, Judas and his brothers successfully contained the Syrian forces in Palestine. It is probable that the Syrians had little money or energy to invest in the battles against the Maccabees in any case. They were occupied with fighting the Parthians in the east and containing Rome's advance from the west. On the 25th Kislev (the ninth month of the Jewish year) 164, Judas managed to enter the temple and rededicate the altar. The worship of Yahweh was technically restored; but the Maccabees were not successful in winning the war. The Syrians held fast to their fortified position and finally struck a deal with the Jews: worship of Yahweh in exchange for acknowledgment of Syrian sovereignty. Although Judas and his brothers Jonathan and Simon are remembered as heroes, their primary contribution was to pacify the *chasidim,* the pious Jews who worried about the purity of the temple cult and the priesthood, and to keep the burden of taxation light. Skirmishes between Syrian and Maccabean forces continued for the next twenty years as did contention over the priesthood .

Following the death of Judas, his brother Simon received certain concessions from the Syrians; minted his own coins; and assumed the offices of high priest, commander of the army, leader of Jerusalem and dynastic patriarch. In fact, by the year 140 the Hasmonean dynasty had become infected with the Hellenistic temperament of Jerusalem itself. Whatever its original interest, as a rural guerrilla movement, in restoring the worship of Yahweh in Jerusalem, its dynastic ambition as reflected in Simon's Pooh-Bah approach to government, finance and religion repelled many of the *chasidim* who had supported the Maccabean tax and temple revolt. From the time of Jonathan onward a steady stream of Jews "exiled" themselves in the Judaean desert in opposition to the "wicked priest"— either Alkimus (d. 160) or perhaps Simon himself. These *Essenes*, whose habits are described by the Jewish historian Josephus, are now widely thought to be identical to the Dead Sea community at Khirbet Qumran. Whatever else their exodus may have represented, it betokened sharp opposition to the power politics of the Hasmoneans. The portrait of the "restoration of Judaism" under Simon given in 1 Macc. 14.8–15, where he is seen as a messiah figure and the fulfillment of prophecy (cf. Mic. 4.4.) cannot be true to the slovenly religious environment of late second-century B.C.E. Jerusalem.

Simon was murdered by an Egyptian assassin in 134. He was succeeded by his son John Hyrcanus, who managed to extend the power base of the Jewish kingdom. Using mercenaries along with local troops, Hyrcanus invaded Samaria and demolished the ancient temple on Mount Gerizim, the "rival" to the temple in Jerusalem, and in 107 conquered and devastated Samaria itself. He thrust into Idumea (Edom) and flogged the local population into submission, "converting" them *en masse* to Judaism. Oddly, or perhaps not, these exploits do not seem to have been undertaken for religious reasons, and they were forthrightly rejected in pious Jewish circles. The Pharisees loudly disapproved of Hyrcanus' tactics, accusing him of behaving like the Antiochene kings he had opposed. Land-grabs were undertaken for prestige value, not in the interest of extending God's kingdom on earth, though the latter rationale was used to defend the adventures. The Sadducees were slightly more sympathetic than the Pharisees, the latter demanding that Hyrcanus give up the office of high priest on the reckoning that—as his mother had been imprisoned and probably raped by the Syrians—he might well be illegitimate and thus unfit for the task.

The further history of the Maccabees down to 107 is a "typical" history of dynastic infighting. On the death of Hyrcanus, rule was seized by his son Aristobolus, who promptly arranged for his brother Antigonus' assassination, the imprisonment of his other brothers, and the isolation of his mother, whom Hyrcanus had appointed to rule in his stead. If the names chosen by the Maccabees tell us anything about the religious temper of the times, it is clear that the Hasmoneans of the first century B.C.E. regarded themselves as the "Jewish" heirs of Alexander. Although they were not equipped to take on the superpowers of the Hellenistic world, they mimicked the Seleucid (Syrian) and Ptolemaic (Egyptian) kings in style, manners, and military bravado.

When Aristobolus died in 103 B.C.E., his wife, Salome Alexandra, freed her husband's brothers from prison and married Jonathan, the eldest. Jonathan thereupon changed his name to Alexander Jannaeus; after finishing his brother's subjugation of Galilee, Jordan and the Mediterranean coast, he thrust into the kingdom of the Nabataeans. Judaism was now imposed on the conquered peoples with boys and men required to undergo circumcision at swordpoint.

Unlike the nations who had accepted Hellenism and had learned to admire Greek civilization in its devolved form, the territories conquered by the later Maccabees deeply resented their Hellenized Jewish masters. And for their part, rulers like Jannaeus found the loyalty of the Samaritans and Galileans impossible to command. Worse, the *chasidim* in Jerusalem thought of Jannaeus as a Greek in Jew's clothing. He had disgraced the temple and the priesthood in insisting on retaining the office of high priest throughout his military exploits, returning to Jerusalem only long enough to wash the blood from his hands. On one occasion, Jannaeus brought 800 rebels back to Jerusalem, herded them through the town, then arranged a great feast for his lieutenants and concubines in a makeshift arena where the rebels were crucified. Once the crosses had been pulled aloft, the wives and children of the victims were brought to the foot of the crosses and were slain before the eyes of the crucified men.

ROME

By the time Salome Alexandra died in 67 B.C.E., the weakened and economically exhausted kingdom of the Seleucids had been incorporated into the Roman Empire as the province of Syria.

Palestine would soon follow, after token opposition by Aristobolus II, Salome's ambitious and ill-tempered son. After a three-month siege the Roman general Pompey entered the temple and inspected the Holy of Holies, while the *chasidim* waited breathlessly to see whether this inspection would be a repetition of the Seleucid "abomination" of 167—the introduction of swine sacrifice and the abolition of the cult of Yahweh. Despicable and religiously marginal as the Hasmoneans had been, they had at least managed to protect the cult: the worship of Yahweh had survived alongside some highly questionable practices of distinctly non-Jewish origin. The Maccabees would soon join Abraham and Moses as pillars of Jewish nostalgia, though their excesses would also be remembered.

The best guess is that in entering the temple, the Romans did not wish to antagonize the feuding Jewish sects of Pharisees, Sadducees and others. They wanted loyalty and stability. The reaction of the pious at the time was to blame the whole affair on Jewish apostasy rather than on the Romans: "The sinners [Romans] insolently knocked down the strong walls with battering rams, and You, Lord, did not stop them. The strangers [Romans] approached your altar and walked on it with their shoes, because the sons of Jerusalem desecrated the sanctuary and defiled God's sacrifice in godlessness" (*Psalms of Solomon* 2.1–3). Although the reference may be to Aristobolus' unworthy tenure as high priest, the impression that mini-sanctuaries to foreign gods and sacrificial cults had flourished throughout the dying days of Hasmonean rule, just as they had before the fall of Jerusalem to the Babylonians, is unavoidable. Aristobolus II and his sons Alexander and Antigonus were brought as prisoners to Rome A puling Hyrcanus II, who had been ousted from the high priesthood, was reinstalled.

"From Babylon to Rome," the history of Judah is a story of political instability and religious compromise. While the biblical story is remarkably clear in this respect, biblical mythology and theologically driven history have tended to see the same half millennium as a story of the survival of monotheistic faith against the strong odds that it would perish, a victim of the infidel cultures that encroached upon it. St. Paul would later summarize this history as an impossible attempt to keep laws that could not be kept, but which grew in number and rigor with each new priestly generation that could not keep them. The self-blame, the anguish, and religious *angst* engendered by the feeling that God was more often on the side of the stranger than of his own faithless people is a crucial part of this history, and it is well known that the prophets were not above raising poignant questions about the justice of this God (Jer. 8.18–22). But the answers that are reckoned to carry divine authority are echoes of the prophets' voices: "Why do [my people] provoke me with their images and foreign gods. . . . Adulterers are they all, a mob of traitors" (Jer. 8.19.2). The prophets might well talk about laws being written in the heart and not on stone, but even in Jesus' day, it was the law that was credited with staying power and that was seen as the essential data of God's revelation to his people.

The law is often seen to float above the heads of worldly events and actors as the proof that Judaism was quintessentially about the worship of the true God even if the Jews, in particular historical and political situations, habitually neglected the divine ordinances and feasts. The "true" story, insofar as it can be separated from the biblical account, is that the ordinances were a part of a struggle to maintain a dying cult against the lures and temptations of more powerful neighbors and empires. Rome was the last culturally imperialist civilization to come into contact with the depleted territory of Judah before its collapse. What survives this collapse religiously speaking is *rabbinical Judaism*, deprived of political power and aspiration, of land and kingship, and of a religious "center" in the form of a temple, and *Christianity*, a Jewish messianic sect, which begins in an equally stateless fashion but acquires Rome itself in the process of its development.

What survives, therefore, is not a coherent theological vision—that had been made politically untenable—but the law, understood to be a coherent prescription for righteousness in the eyes of a fundamentally righteous God.

In 57 B.C.E. the Roman provincial governor Gabinius split Palestine into five administrative units. Judaea was divided into three sectors: Jerusalem, Gazara and Jericho, while Galilee was united with the district of Sepphoris and Perea to the district of Amanthus. The divisions were designed to fracture Jewish nationalism, which whimsically vacillated between supporting Pompey and supporting Julius Caesar prior to Pompey's murder in Egypt in 48 B.C.E. The surviving Hasmonean, Hyrcanus, and Antipater switched their allegiance quickly to the victorious side; as a reward Caesar guaranteed the rights of the cultic community in Jerusalem with Hyrcanus as high priest and "ethnarch"—a specially forged title—of Jerusalem and Joppa.

Antipater was named an honorary Roman citizen and procurator of Judaea—essentially a Roman civil servant put in place to inform the Romans of any suspicious goings-on among the rival Jewish sects. The move was not, at first, regarded as an outrage. Antipater was an Idumean, after all: an outsider but still technically "Jewish." The office he occupied, however, was effectively that of governor and administrator, and his loyalties were to Rome, not to the Jews. He acted in typical Maccabean fashion by ensuring a succession of like-minded administrators in the persons of his sons, Phaesel and Herod. Herod was given the territory of Galilee to administer; Phaesel ruled Judaea.

Herod acted decisively to rid Galilee of the "bandits," i.e., nationalistic Jewish partisans who had opposed Roman rule at the time of Judaea's subjugation. While he won applause from Rome for this cleanup operation, the Sanhedrin—the legislative and judicial body to whom life-and-death questions should have been referred—was outraged. When they called Herod to account for his summary execution of the bandits, he appeared, surrounded by bodyguards. The Sanhedrin were reminded how puny their power really was when confronted by an agent of Roman interests and Roman justice. In the time of Jesus, the Jerusalem *synedrion*'s religious police had the right to arrest those charged with not keeping the law, but in matters involving the life and death of the accused, it was obliged to submit its action for the review of Roman authorities.

The power struggle that affected the empire between 44 and 37 following the murder of Julius Caesar ended with Herod alone in a bargaining position. He fled to Rome to make his case against rival claimants to power and was rewarded for his political sense with the title "King of the Jews" and Roman forces to help him win back his "kingdom" from Antigonus, the last of the pure-bred Hasmoneans. He was reconfirmed in this office after having switched allegiance from Marc Antony to Octavian (Caesar Augustus) following Antony's defeat at Actium in 31 B.C.E.

To secure the support of the surviving Hasmoneans and their sympathizers, Herod married into the old royal family, though he was never able to exorcise his fear that the family would again seize control and reestablish the Jewish state; hence, following the ritual mutilation of the old Hyrcanus (his ears were cut off so that he could not fulfill the office of high priest) he decided that the old man should be murdered. In his place Herod installed his wife's brother, Aristobolus, also of the royal lineage. When he grew suspicious of him, Herod hired murderers to kill him in his bath. This was followed by his ordering the murder of his own wife, Mariamne, and two of their sons. Only his firstborn, Herod Antipater, was spared—until just before Herod's death, when even Antipater was accused of treachery and sentenced to die. Although stories of Jesus' birth in the New Testament are fraught with legend, the story of the slaughter of the male children recounted in Matt. 2.16 is a legend informed by contemporary assessments of Herod's character.

Religiously, Herod was suspected of being soft on paganism. His kingdom included Jews and Greeks, and he tried hard to be each to all. He failed. His sympathies were decidedly Greek and the tastes he cultivated originated in Rome. His inner circle consisted mainly of educated Hellenists, political advisors, philosophers, musicians and architects. His domestic policy was focused on building Greek cities throughout his territory, with baths, gymnasia, and theaters. And like a good Roman patron, he promoted the pagan cults with an active program that included the building of temples to adorn the new cities. As a consolation to his more pious clients, Herod arranged for the enlargement of the temple in Jerusalem (a project not complete in Jesus' day: cf. Mark 13.1) and respected the wishes of the priests that the sanctuary be covered at all times during the remodeling.

Herod's real effort was invested in proving himself a worthy, if somewhat junior, successor to Alexander. On the site of the ruined city of Samaria he created a new city in honor of Augustus, Sebaste ("The Exalted"), and on the coast he built a modern harbor-town and named it Caesarea. In Jerusalem itself he erected a fortress, the Antonia, located directly on the temple square where he could keep constant surveillance of the temple construction site, and on the western shore of the Dead Sea he built an almost impregnable fortification, Masada, set on top of a mountain. In the style of a Latin patron, Herod was eager to display his wealth and to guarantee his prestige.

JOHN AND THE BAPTISTS

According to the gospels, toward the end of Herod's life (4 B.C.E.) Jesus of Nazareth and John the Baptist were born (Matt. 2.1; Luke 1.5). The latter appears to have belonged to a radical sect of Jewish dissidents who, while opposed to the Herodians and to Roman domination of the Jewish state, advocated separation from mainstream Judaism as the only way to achieve a measure of religious purity. Their central sacrament was baptism, which was seen as a sign of repentance not only for the national apostasy represented by the Herodians, but also for the priesthood and the Pharisees. It is useless, if tempting, to speculate on their connections with the Qumran or Dead Sea Community. First-century Judaea was filled with apocalyptic prophets; the bandits were still active, along with shadowy groups like the Sicarii and the religio-political Zealots, each of which represented slightly different solutions to the political reality of Roman occupation.

Most felt powerless to deal with the problem in their midst; thus, solutions ranged from random assassinations carried out against apostate Jews, spies, and Jewish civil servants on the Roman payroll ("publicans") to capitulation, in the case of the Herodian party. The apocalyptic preachers such as John tended to see Jewish history as a story of irreversible decline, at the end of which God would come (or send his delegate, the Son of Man) to judge the gentiles and the unrepentant for their sins. John the Baptist belonged to this tradition. Alongside this solution, however, stood the "preferred" belief that God had not deserted his people and did not intend to settle accounts on a supernatural level. Instead, he would send a *mashiah*, a leader like David, a prophet like Moses—a kingly deliverer who would redeem the nation from its enemies, restore the kingdom, regather the ancient tribes—or such remnants as had remained faithful, wherever they might be—and rule in peace and justice, like Augustus.

Taken literally, the two beliefs seem incompatible: would God save his people by destroying the world, or save the world by delivering his people? But messianic belief and apocalyptic belief were seldom distinctly separated in the popular mind. Many Jews believed in both divine judgment and messianic deliverance, and invented an ingenious literature to bring the two beliefs into conjunction. The remnants of this effort can be seen as early as the Book of Daniel in the Old Testament, but include apocryphal sources like First Enoch, 4 Esdras, as well as the canonical Christian gospels, which belong in part to the literary world of apocalyptic thought (cf. Mark 13; Matt. 25.31–46).

JESUS

The pessimism of previous decades concerning what Jesus of Nazareth might have taught has now largely been set aside by developments in our understanding of the social and religious matrix of first-century Palestine. After John clashed with the Herodian party (Matt. 14.1–12), he was imprisoned in the fortress of Machereus by the Dead Sea (Josephus, *Antiquities* 18.2), and subsequently beheaded. Some of his followers continued to plague the Herodians with their purist interpretations of Judaism (Matt. 9.14) and their insistence on a baptism of "renunciation" or repentance (John 3.22). After his beheading, there was a rumor that John had risen from the dead (Mark 6.16). Some of his followers declared John the messiah and continued to follow a more or less rigorist interpretation of his teaching (Matt. 9.11f.). A slightly more liberal element, though one equally imbued with the spirit of apocalyptic enthusiasm, followed Jesus of Nazareth who declared himself, or was declared (John 1.37), the Baptist's successor. Jesus modified John's ethnocentric message of repentance and judgment (Luke 3.7-9) while building on his radical interpretation of the law (Matt. 5.17-20) and attacks on the Pharisees and (perhaps also) the Herodians (Matt. 22.16; Mark 12.13; 3.6). With the death of Jesus, the cult blended the strands of apocalyptic and messianic thinking to a degree then unparalleled in first-century Judaism. The crucified and defeated messiah would come again as deliverer and judge—the victorious son of man.

Apparently Jesus declared the Pharisees beyond the scope of salvation for their interpretations of the law (Matt. 5.20), which tended to focus on technical requirements rather than personal conversion. The triumph of rabbinical Judaism after the destruction of the temple and the obliteration of the priesthood in 70 C.E. (which was a triumph for legal interpretation in the pharisaic style) marginalized Jesus' apocalyptic teaching to such an extent that early preachers like Paul had little option but to declare the law "fulfilled" in Jesus, a view then read back into the preaching of Jesus himself (Matt. 5.17-18).

Around the time of John's arrest it would seem that a dispute ensued about the meaning of baptism, John's followers declaring that those who wished to escape divine retribution should be washed as a token of their repentance. Jesus' followers, meanwhile, claimed that the baptism was a "spiritual" preparation for the dawning of God's kingdom—a spiritual rebirth (John 3.8). Jesus' message of apocalyptic judgment was, at the outset, no different from John's (Mark 1.14). His early followers were disposed to look upon him as being—in some sense—the fulfillment of John's gospel of repentance, and only with difficulty were they able to separate his message from that of their original prophet. By the time Jesus removed himself from Galilee, having run afoul of popular feeling there (Mark 6.5), his followers had begun to think of him as a prophet in his own right, associating his rejection and defeat with the unwillingness of Israel to listen to the prophets who had come before (Mark 8.28).

The New Testament tradition also preserves the belief that Jesus was the messiah or *christos*, i.e., the anointed one of God who would restore the kingdom of Israel and defeat the enemies of God. Jesus' followers evidently included, besides the legendary twelve members of both theological and political camps, those who saw him as the prefigurement of an apocalyptic judge and those who saw him as a political savior. It *may* have included members of the Zealot party and members of the Sicarii, the assassins, if the names Simon the Zealot and Judas Iscariot are of historical significance.

The two competing but often indistinguishable traditions—messianic and apocalyptic—in popular Judaism merged into a single grand scheme in the gospels. Jesus was viewed as *both* son of man and messiah, the lord (king) Christ and savior; the son of God and prophet like Moses; the son of David, who would come again in glory to redeem the nation. In the Hellenistic preaching of the gospel, however, these "titles" were quickly decontextualized and subsumed within the widespread belief that Jesus was a savior god on the order of Asklepios and Mithras, despite the efforts of the preachers to keep this belief under control (Phil. 2.5-11).

This speculation took place against the background of rabbinical Judaism and an emasculated priesthood, not to mention a puppet Herodian dynasty that had to bear the insult of having a Roman governor deciding cases which, in better days, would have been decided directly by Jewish authorities.

The tradition that Jesus was betrayed by Jews in his own party and crucified by the Romans as part of a conspiracy is not fashionable. It remains, however, the most plausible explanation of the events leading to his death and is fully supported by the evidence of the gospels and non-Christian sources. According to the gospel tradition (Mark 14.50), not only Judas and Peter but the whole band of disciples deserted Jesus at the time of his arrest. Later attempts to rehabilitate the apostles through a post-resurrection "enlightenment" and the descent of the spirit on the feast of Pentecost bear the traces of second-century legend (cf. Acts 2.3): Its function was to ensure that the deserters become official witnesses and teachers of a new messianic faith through the divine charism, the gift of the "holy spirit."

The facts are probably more mundane. Jesus ran afoul of the Pharisees for his style of legal interpretation; of the Sadducees for his (apparent) contempt for the temple cult and perhaps also because of his origins; and of his own followers, or the bandits and zealots among them, for failing to liberate the Jewish nation from the yoke of foreign domination (cf. Luke 24.21). This is three-pronged Jewish opposition which could be resolved only through assassination or judicial despatch. While scholars clash on this point, the judicial process involved seems to have belonged to the Romans, since a sentence of death was officially requested by the Jewish opponents. By the same token, the mob scenes (cf. Matt. 27.24-26) with the "Jews" begging Pilate for crucifixion and Pilate washing his hands of an innocent man's blood "in full view of the people," are self-serving fictions designed, insofar as possible, to remove the burden of guilt from the Roman protectors, upon whose unpredictable good will the Christian missionaries depended for the continuation of their mission. The crucifixion of Jesus from the standpoint of both sides was not an injustice but an agreement to remove a difficult character from public view. There was nothing complicated about such an arrangement.

Whether Jesus preached against the paying of taxes to the Romans or offended the priests with his not-so-veiled threat against the temple cult (Mark 11.17f.) cannot be decided. The actions of Pilate in "handing Jesus over" are in general alignment with the picture of the governor painted by Josephus. Pilate would not have been interested in the "theological" correctness of Jesus' position, but he would have gone out of his way to prevent an uprising instigated by an alliance of Pharisees, Sadducees, and disappointed Zealots.

What seems to have regathered Jesus' followers out of their retreat in Galilee was the "news" of his resurrection, a tale parallel to that originally circulated about John the Baptist. Jewish polemic immediately countered (Matt. 28.14-15) that Jesus' disciples had stolen his body. By this time, however, conflicting tales of Jesus' appearances—to disciples in Galilee, to pilgrims along the road, to Mary of Magdala outside the tomb, to crowds in and around Jerusalem—had begun to circulate wildly and continued for years after his death (1 Cor. 15.3–7). Jesus' last "public" appearance prior to his arrest, a Sabbath and possibly a Passover meal with his followers, became saturated with reminiscence and remembered promises: he had said he would die; he had predicted that he would rise; he had told his disciples that he would be away for a little while but had said he would come again. Slowly his life story began to take shape against the promises of apocalyptic fulfillment and the Jewish docrine of the Son of Man. Past disappointment gave way to the hope of Jesus' quick return, a hope enhanced by a growing conviction that God had raised him from the dead because he was God's own son, the chosen one of Israel (Acts 2.22–36).

The New Testament presents this evidence in the context of a "salvation history" whereby prophecies after the fact are given as foreshadowings of a divine plan (e.g., Ps. 16.8–11). From the standpoint of a social and cultural history of the movement, however, there is little doubt that the attractive thing about Jesus of Nazareth was not his bizarre apocalyptic predictions, which after a while had been softened to the point of melting. It was rather the belief that Jesus had been raised from the dead and the good news that the same fate awaited those who believed that he saved them from "sin and death," which had acquired a cause/effect relationship in early Christian preaching (1 Cor. 15.12–19). It was this message, enhanced by the teaching of the Greek salvation cults and augmented increasingly by "sayings" attributed to Jesus and "signs" he had performed as enticements to belief in him, that formed the nucleus of the gospel tradition.

NOTICES AND CRITIQUES OF THE NEW FAITH

The criticism of the resurrection faith was almost immediate, beginning with Jewish accusations that the followers of Jesus had fabricated the story of his resurrection (Matt. 27.15; 1 Cor. 15.14). This accusation passed quickly from rabbinical discussion to gentile ears and pivoted on two contingent pieces of information: first, no one—not even Jesus' followers—had witnessed the resurrection. Early on the Christians were hard pressed to deny this fact, and the earliest of the gospel reports, that of Mark, exhausts the primitive tradition by declaring that a group of women, finding empty the place where Jesus' body had been laid, ran away in terror to report the news to his confused (male) disciples in Galilee, where they had fled to avoid arrest.

No effort was made to alter this tradition, apparently, until Jewish speculation concerning the whereabouts of the body made it necessary to offer proof that the body of Jesus had been raised, not stolen and buried privately. The appearance stories grew in number and variety, careless of detail and geographical consistency. Paul knew a tradition current in the 50s and probably before, that Jesus had appeared to Peter (Cephas), the twelve (the number would have to include Judas), five hundred others, followed by James and finally to Paul (1 Cor. 15.4-7). What Paul does with exaggerated numbers Matthew does with literary hyperbole: Guards were posted by the Jews, with Pilate's approval; the tomb was sealed (Matt. 28.66). At daybreak on the Sabbath, however, an earthquake announced the descent of an angel, who broke the seal, opened the tomb, sat on the stone and declared Christ risen to the visitants, while the guards "shook with fear and lay like dead men" (Matt. 28.4).

The Gospel of John adds a male witness at the foot of the cross ("the beloved disciple") and makes this disciple race a disbelieving Peter to the tomb, to find neither Jesus nor an angel (John 20.2-9). The tales of Jesus' appearances following the resurrection—the most famous of which involves an apostle named Thomas or "the Twin" inserting his fingers into the wounds of the risen Lord—were similarly devised to "prove" the resurrection to nay-sayers of assorted varieties.

THE MESSIANIC PROBLEM

The second level of criticism of the resurrection faith was more parochial, at least from the standpoint of Roman perceptions

of the affair. While gentiles were free to believe or disbelieve
the preaching of the resurrection, they were less familiar with
the hopes for the messiah and the disputes between Jews and
Christians that surrounded it. Put bluntly, Jesus lacked the
curriculum vitae of a messiah. He was from a region known
as the *Galil'ha goyim* (i.e., Galilee) whose reputation for religious and ethnic mixing—apostasy in the minds of some
Jerusalemites—was well established (cf. John 1.46). Jewish
tradition and later pagan critics knew Jesus as the son of a
woman named Miriam or Miriamne, who had been violated
and become pregnant by a Roman soldier whose name often
appears as Panthera in talmudic and midrashic sources. The
"single parent" tradition, if not the story of Jesus' illegitimacy,
is still apparent in Mark, the earliest gospel (Mark 6.3), as
is an early attempt to show Jesus' freedom from the blemish
of his background (Mark 3.33-4).

Late first- or early second-century tradition, however, took
the same aggressive stance against Jewish reports concerning
Jesus' birth and lineage as it did against the attacks on the resurrection. Editors of Matthew and Luke contrived genealogies
designed to show that Jesus was descended from the requisite
messianic stock, a true son of David. According to these improvised traditions, he had been born in Bethlehem—a place
named by the prophets as the provenance of the future king
and deliverer (Mic. 5.2). To counter the reports of Jesus' illegitimacy more than to secure his divine stature, his mother was
declared the recipient of a singular divine honor: Jesus was the
son of Mary—a virgin—"through the holy spirit" (Matt. 1.20).
As is typical of his writing, Matthew comes closest to revealing
the argumentative purpose of his birth story and its links to
Jewish polemic against Christian belief in his reference to Joseph's
suspicion of Mary's pregnancy (Matt. 1.19). He is also careful
in the birth story and elsewhere to provide evidence and proofs
from the Septuagint, the Greek translation of the Hebrew bible—
as a running part of his narrative. Almost certainly, the texts
Matthew uses, such as Isa. 7.14 ("A virgin [*parthenos* in Greek,
although the original Hebrew means simply "girl"] shall conceive
and bear a son . . .") were already favorite talking points in
debates between Christian preachers and the rabbis.

Attached to the question of messianic credentials, which loomed large in early Jewish-Christian debate, was the related question of Jesus' fate or, more exactly, the fate of the messiah. One might be able to finesse if not erase a man's origins among the second-class Jews of Galilee; indeed, for some antagonists of the new cult, being from Galilee was slander enough, tantamount to being a bastard ("the son of a carpenter," Mark 6.3). That Jewish polemic is any more "factual" in this respect than Christian attempts to evade the slander is doubtful.

But the crucifixion of Jesus was a public event. *That* Jesus was executed is agreed upon by Jewish and Christian traditions, and more significantly perhaps by such "outsiders" as Josephus and Tacitus. Traditions preserved in the non-Christian sources differed, however. According to Tacitus, writing around 115 C.E., Jesus was "executed in Tiberius' reign by the governor of Judaea, Pontius Pilate" (*Annals* 15.43). But in talmudic literature we find the following: "This they did to Jeshu ben Stada [Jesus] in Lud: two disciples of the wise were chosen for him, and they brought him to the Beth Din [place of judgment] and stoned him" (T.Sanh. X.11 and J. Sanh. 7.16/25c,d). In the Jewish tradition, which, measured against the chronology of the gospels and pagan sources, is full of anachronisms, the charges against Jesus were sorcery, the preaching of heresy, and leading the "whole world astray" (cf. Luke 23.2f.).

The Jewish tradition is driven by the conviction that Jesus had not been the messiah—a question of little relevance to writers like Tacitus. His judicial killing according to the penalty described for a heretic and magician (b. Sanh. 43a) served as a proof that he had not been God's anointed, the deliverer of his people. A Roman execution would, according to the law, have left the matter undecided; hence, in the Jewish polemical tradition Jesus was stoned and thereby proved to be a false messiah bent on leading his people into the worship of false gods. He is equated elsewhere with Ahab, Jeroboam and Manesseh—the kings who presided over the apostasy of Israel and Judah.

More difficult to explain, from the Christian side, was the death of their messiah in humiliating circumstances, deserted by his closest followers. There were very few, if any, references to a Christ who would fail spectacularly to achieve the this-worldly hopes of the nation. Indeed the term was used specifically to denote kingly heroism, military prowess and success, as its application to the Persian king Cyrus (Isa. 45.1) suggests. The term presupposed not only ancient Davidic lineage (Mic. 5.2–5) but also one who would restore and uphold the kingdom of David forever (Isa. 9.6–7). Jewish polemic was severe on this point: Jesus had failed, as had Theudas, a magician named by Josephus (*Antiquities* 20.5.1) as having attracted a following (beheaded ca. 44 during the procuratorship of Fadus), and Judas, another Galilean "messiah" mentioned by Josephus (*Antiquities* 18.1.1; cf. Acts 5.36f.) as having raised an insurrection over the enrollment ca. 4 B.C.E. Between the time of Theudas and the bar Kochba rebellion of 132 C.E. Judaism had grown suspicious of pretenders to the messianic title. Insofar as any claim of the sort was made on Jesus' behalf during his lifetime, the Jews of the city would have been suspicious of the "Galileans" as well (Acts 5.27–40).

FROM THE TEMPLE TO BAR KOCHBA

The messianic movement associated with bar Kochba in the second century, though later in point of origin than Christianity, provides the most edifying parallel to the Christian movement. The Hellenistic cities created by the Herods had become hotbeds of Jewish and Greek tension. Anti-Jewish demonstrations broke out repeatedly in Caesarea and reached such intensity that the Jewish inhabitants of the city were reduced to paying protection money to the Romans. When the Romans failed to respond effectively to put down the riots, scattered resistance to their misrule and partisan support for the Hellenists turned into armed rebellion. In Jerusalem the temple area was seized by the Zealot leader John of Gischala, the rest of Jerusalem by Simon bar Giora. After a series of shows of force, the Romans under Titus broke through the city walls on three sides, set fire to the temple, and managed to wrest from the holy of holies its seven-branched candlestick and the table of the unleavened bread, which were taken as trophies back to Rome along with the rebel leaders. The destruction of the temple meant the end of the Sadducean party. The Pharisees concentrated their energies on the developing synagogue movement, since with the burning of the temple the sacrificial cult had come to an end. The synagogues were under the protection of the civil authorities, and were left alone to develop a new and distinctive style of Judaism so long as they did not become centers for political discussion, and dutifully paid to Rome the tax which previously had been collected from Jews for the maintenance of the temple.

On a routine tour of the eastern province of Palestine in 130, the emperor Hadrian decreed that a temple to the Roman god Jupiter should be built on the site of Herod's ruined temple. In an unrelated edict, Hadrian ordered a stop to the practice of ritual castration, a ban which was understood to include the rite of circumcision. A rebellion against the decrees, led by a certain Simon bar Kochba (or bar Cosiba) succeeded in regaining Judah and Jerusalem. Sacrifices were offered on the temple site and coins were minted as a sign of "independence" from Rome, using the first year of the rebellion as beginning of the new era. Rabbi Akiba, one of the foremost biblical interpreters of the day, declared bar Kochba the promised messiah, the "son of the daystar" spoken of in Num. 24.17. Since the Jewish Christians in Palestine could not accept bar Kochba's messianic claims, they were pursued and bloodily persecuted if they refused to renounce Jesus as the messiah (Justin, *Apology* 1.31).

The Romans closed in slowly, forced to find the rebels in their hiding places. Bar Kochba entrenched himself in Beth-Ter in Judah, surrounded by his closest followers, but the Romans had little difficulty in breaching his defenses. His slaying by the Romans was seen as a compelling disproof of his messiahship, and rabbinical Judaism seldom referred to him thereafter by name. The rabbis who had sided with bar Kochba were executed; Akiba himself is said to have had his flesh raked with iron combs before being put to death. On the ruins of Jerusalem, Hadrian's "model city," Colonia Aelia Capitolina, was erected. A temple dedicated to Jupiter was constructed, and Jews were forbidden to enter the city.

CHRISTS AND CHRISTIC TITLES

The oblivion that encircled "false" messiahs from Theudas to bar Kochba did not touch Jesus of Nazareth. Three strands of argument and belief were woven together to prevent him from falling into obscurity. These can be summarized as (1) the belief in the resurrection, (2) the Christian use and interpretation of prophecy, and (3) Christological complexity of the movement's understanding of Jesus' person and work. These cannot be dealt with in detail here, but any understanding of the strokes and angles of later criticism of Christian doctrine and practice depends on knowing that from its earliest days, the church was an "apologetic" structure. This means simply that doctrines which are usually thought to be the defining ones of Christianity developed in an environment hostile to Jesus' messianic claims, beginning with the view that he lacked the Davidic credentials to fulfill the role, and ending with the view that his death was—like bar Kochba's—sufficient disproof of his followers' preaching. The pagan critics later embraced this fundamentally Jewish view enthusiastically.

The Christian missionary preaching of the mid-to-late first century C.E. was summarized by Paul's assurances that "Jesus, the messiah, is Lord" (Phil. 2.11). The proof of this was his resurrection, the overcoming of death, which, in line with Jewish atonement theology, was also seen as a conquest of sin by the incarnation of innocence or righteousness in the person of Jesus himself. He was the perfectly righteous victim, the spotless lamb of God, who took the sins of the world onto himself. Thus his death was the "climax" of the temple cult (on the verge of collapse when this theology developed). He could be called "high priest" and, with tortured logic, the "sacrificial victim"—a "spiritual and eternal sacrifice" (Heb. 9.14) whose blood washed away corruption.

The death of Jesus could be frankly acknowledged, therefore, as a "moment" in a process, at the end of which stood the negation of death (1 Cor. 15.20-1). In this way, the historical data—the failure of the messianic mission in this worldly terms—were overturned by the belief that only one *part* of the mission had been fulfilled. The momentous events, beginning with a resurrection known only to his closest followers, was still to come and would be made known to all only in the "last days" (cf. Mark 13. 26-7). By then, however, it would be too late for the enemies of the gospel to repent and to accept Jesus as Lord, a calculation which introduced the element of threat into the call for conversion. Who Jesus had been would be made known unmistakably in the future—a future calculated by using the standard symbols of Jewish apocalyptic thought. This amalgamation may have been more a confusion of images than a studied blueprint for converting masses to the new faith, but all the religions of the empire, from Judaism to the gnostic schools and mystery cults, were amalgamations of some sort.

In an obvious way, this stratum of messianic "proof" was untestable. No one could say precisely *when* the effects of the resurrection would be made known unmistakably or when Jesus would be revealed from heaven as the true savior of the nation and the world. Even the gospels and letters of Paul were remarkably indefinite about the timing of these events (cf. Mark 9.1; 13. 31-32; 1 Thess. 5.2f.). The hope of the small community, of course, was that the proof would come "soon" (1 Cor. 16.22), especially as expulsions from the synagogues of the empire exposed clutches of Christians to the discipline of Roman judges and to the contempt of the intellectual classes.

A related and more testable assertion was the claim that the death of the messiah had been prophesied and that, therefore, the death of Jesus conformed to Jewish messianic expectation. The resurrection would have been—in terms of messianic claims, anyway—an unnecessary addition to the Christian armory of proofs and cases if the tradition of a dying messiah could be maintained. Attention fell on the book of Isaiah as a storehouse of rabbinical speculation concerning the messiah. Isa. 53 (52.13-53.12), commonly known today as "the fourth servant song," speaks of a nation despised, tormented by its enemies, pierced, chastised, and tortured by God for the unfaithfulness of the people. The nation is Israel, personified as a suffering servant who is buried among the wicked but who will one day be restored (healed) by God and vindicated for having made itself a sacrifice for sin. In Christian interpretation, the story of Israel was dislocated from its historical context and applied to the life history of Jesus. The servant was Jesus not Israel; the restoration referred not to the political welfare of the nation but to the resurrection and reappearance of the Christ. The crucifixion narratives were actually constructed with the text of Isa. 53, Ps. 22, and perhaps the apocryphal Wisdom of Solomon 2.10–24 in hand as "prooftexts" in support of the claim that the messiah was ordained to die an ugly and seemingly meaningless death—from which he would be rescued as a sign that he had redeemed others.

These texts would have been compelling had the Jews recognized them as "messianic" and if the idea of a dying and rising messiah had occurred in first-century Judaism. During the reign of Hadrian, it is true, certain rabbis seem to have read Deut. 33.16 (Moses' blessing of Joseph) as having to do with a kind of "proto-messiah" who would die in a victorious encounter with Gog and Magog (the powers of evil) after a glorious career. There was no notion that this figure would suffer, nor that his death would have a redemptive significance. By the same token, Isa. 53 was not taken by the Jews of Jesus' generation to refer to the messiah or to announce his coming. In his "Dialogue with Trypho," written toward the end of the second century, Justin Martyr strives to persuade his Jewish opponent that the death of Christ was foretold in prophecy. Trypho—Justin's invention and his ideally agreeable opponent—acknowledges the "truth" of most of what Justin has to say, with one exception: "Whether the messiah should be shamefully crucified, this we are in doubt about; for whoever is crucified is said to be accursed by the law. I am exceedingly incredulous on this point" (*Dialogue with Trypho* 89). Justin proceeds to put together a tangle of texts, including a reflection on Deut. 33.13–17, which may have influenced rabbinical thinking on the point. But it was only in conversation with Christian teachers that some texts acquired a messianic gloss. At the time the gospels were composed, the death of the messiah caused confusion (Mark 8.32; Matt. 16.22) and could only be substantiated on the testimony of the risen Jesus (Luke 24.46) or attributed to a deliberate design of God (Acts 2.23f; Eph. 3.9–13). An early Christian sermon defended the death of the Christ as the amortization of the devil's lease on the world, the canceling of a debt owed by God to Evil: "[God] has forgiven us of all our sins; he has canceled the bond which pledged us to the terms of the law. It stood against us but he has set it aside, nailing it to the cross. On that cross he discarded the cosmic powers [of wickedness] and authorities like a garment; he made a public spectacle of them and led them as captives in his triumphal procession" (Col. 2.14–15). Thus, from the end of the first century onward, the preaching strategy diverted attention from the visible proofs and signs of messiahship to the "unseen" and hence untestable assertion of what his death accomplished on a cosmic scale. It was Jesus' death, interpreted messianically, rather than his life that saved him from obscurity.

A final stratum of defense, which grew naturally out of the diffuseness of early Christian preaching, was the use of multiple titles to refer to Jesus. While the risen Jesus of Luke 24 can declare with authority that the "Messiah is to suffer death and rise from the dead," the earliest recorded "prophecies" of the death of Jesus prior to the crucifixion referred to the death of the "son of Man" (Mark 8.31; 9.13; 10. 34). Traditionally commentary on these passages has focused on the fact that Jesus speaks on these three occasions not of his own ("I must be betrayed and killed") but of the *son of man*'s betrayal and death. In fact, the use of the apocalyptic title—"son of man" instead of messiah—may well have grown out of the need to divert attention from the latter usage.

The political overtones of the messianic claim were so pronounced and the expectations attached to the feats of the messiah so numerous that the gospel of John, in a famous interrogation scene, actually presents Jesus repudiating messiahship: "My kingship is not of this world. If it were, my followers would be fighting to save me from the Jews. . . . 'King' is your word, my task is to bear witness to the truth" (John 16-7). Growing originally out of differing political and theological viewpoints, the son of man and the messiah became in Christianity a single figure: that of the risen and exalted Christ "who would come again." Titles such as "son of God" or "a son of God," "Lord," "son of David," "prophet [like Moses]"

(Acts 3.22) and "servant of God" (after Isa. 53), despite their technical differences, were brought together instinctively in the preaching of the early missionaries. The titles represented at one level a multiple-choice approach to the divinity of Jesus: Jews and Greeks heard different things when confronted with phrases such as "son of God." But at a strategic level the titles could be used in debate as ways of qualifying what was meant, or what was implied, in the eccentric Christian understanding of who the messiah was, what was expected of him, and how his death should be interpreted. While there was nothing deliberate about the logic of this development, the result might be summarized as follows:

- Jesus of Nazareth was the Christ, the son of God
- who was also the son of man and thus God's pre-appointed representative on the day of Judgment;
- who would be revealed in glory on the last day, but whose glory had been hidden during his earthly ministry;
- and who had died in "accordance with scripture" (i.e., prophetic texts) as an atoning sacrifice for the sins—not only of the Jewish people but of the world;
- and who, as the risen Christ, offered the gift of salvation (from sin) and eternal life (its reward) to everyone who believed in him.

Against the view that Jesus failed to conform to Jewish requirements for a messiah the Christian preachers could offer only vague scriptural retorts. An example survives from the late first or early second century in a speech attributed to Peter, and reportedly given in the Court of the Gentiles (the east colonnade of the temple) to a Jewish audience (Acts 3.17-24):

[Men of Israel] This is how God has fulfilled what he had foretold in the utterances of all the prophets: that his messiah should suffer. . . . Repent so that your sins may be wiped out. Then God may grant you a time of recovery and send to you the messiah he had already appointed, that is, Jesus. He must be received into heaven until the time of universal restoration comes, of which God spoke by the holy prophets.

The speech is important not because it can be plausibly ascribed to the apostle Peter (it is given a setting more appropriate to a speech delivered by a Greek rhetor on a public festival), but because it may preserve something of the argumentative thrust of actual preaching by early Jewish and Samaritan missionaries.

By the early second century, the churches of Syria and Palestine had grown more confident of their use and interpretation of prophecy. For the second-century Syrian bishop Ignatius, only those prophecies which corroborated Christian doctrine were to be accounted true, since "Jesus Christ is the door through which the prophets enter the church" (*Ep. to the Philadelphians* 9.1). This inversion made it possible for Christians to appropriate the Old Testament as a preparation for the gospel, though pagan and Jewish observers of the new religion were unsparing in their criticism of applying prophecies, in an exclusive way, to Jesus of Nazareth. Porphyry notes that what is said in Hebrew prophecy could as well apply to a dozen other figures, dead or yet to come, as to Jesus.

JEWS AND CHRISTIANS ADRIFT: FROM NOTICE TO POLEMIC

By the year 100 C.E., the religious split between Jews and Christians had been clearly defined, if not always clearly expressed, in every city or in the minds of Roman observers. Judaism was to continue as a licit religion (*religio licita*), approved if not encouraged by Rome. The problematical temple cult had been destroyed and, with it, the debates over the purity and descent of the priesthood which had plagued ceremonial Judaism since the Captivity. Judaism had lost its center, if not its spirit, but was as much a pilgrim religion in the Roman Empire as the foundling and illegal "congregations" of Christians.

Judaism was not inconsequential to antiquity-conscious Romans. From their standpoint, Jewish civilization, being older than their own, possessed an element of truth: "What is old is true, what is true is old" was a dictum which the Christians struggled to overcome in their efforts to persuade the Romans that their cult was not a discredited sect of Judaism (an opinion urged upon the Romans by Jewish lobbyists in their exclusion of Christian teachers from synagogues, in their ritual curse of the Nazarenes, and in slanderous propaganda such as the ben Panthera tradition). No Christian *littérateur* of the late first century commanded a Roman audience as extensive or influential as the Jewish historian Josephus. Indeed all the letters surviving from the earliest period of Christian history, from Paul to Clement of Rome (ca. 98), are attempts to bring the cult under control and to define the rudiments of its beliefs. It was not the kind of literature—or message—that could have assuaged Roman suspicions that Christianity was, above all, new, unproved, and potentially dangerous.

Josephus had fought against Vespasian toward the beginning of the Jewish war in 68. Suspected by the Jews of being a capitulator, he returned as an observer and court reporter for the final siege in 70 under the Roman commander Titus' protection. After the war, he returned to Rome and was awarded the rights of Roman citizenship for distinguished service as a translator, mediator and chronicler. In his treatise *Against Apion*, Josephus responds to the increasing anti-Semitism of late first-century Rome, a city that was destined to receive masses of Jewish immigrants dispossessed of their homeland between 70 and 135. Written around 94 C.E., with the Christian community itself beginning to make strides, the treatise performed the task of reminding the Romans (thinly disguised in his lecture as the "Greeks") of the antiquity of his own people. The Jews are more ancient than the Greeks, he observes. Egyptians, Phoenicians, and Babylonians all testify to his nation's history, though Greece is not mentioned and indeed is a relative latecomer in world affairs. Moreover, the laws of Moses and the ethical code of the Jews are far superior to the immoral myths of the Greeks and their inferior conceptions of the gods.

Hardly a defense used by Josephus and hardly a charge leveled against the Jews by Roman anti-Semites fails to resurface in the empire's war against the Christian church and its practices. Even Christian martyrdom, seen early on as the sublimest "proof" of the faith, is anticipated in Josephus' defense of the Law: "We have practical proof of our reverence for our own scriptures. For although long ages have now passed, no one has dared to remove or to alter a syllable: and it is an instinct with every Jew from the day of his birth to regard them as the decrees of God, to abide by them and, if need be, cheerfully to die for them. Time and again ere now the sight has been witnessed of prisoners enduring tortures and death in every form in the theaters rather than utter a single word against the law and the allied documents" (*Contra Apionem* 1.42f.). Both Josephus the Jew and Tertullian the Christian (cf. *Apology* 39, 40) make steadfastness and virtue their "proofs" of authenticity. What confessing Jesus as "lord" was to the Christian martyrs, adherence to Moses and the law was to the Jews.

As rabbinical Judaism and Christianity entered onto the Roman scene in harness, the one claiming legitimacy on the basis of history, the other on the basis of having fulfilled Judaism's historical purpose, there was predictable confusion and disarray of opinion. Writing around 115, Tacitus describes the beliefs and traditions of Judaism in a way that suggests the ineffectiveness of Josephus' defense: "[Jewish] customs owe their strength to their very badness. . . . They regard the rest of mankind with hatred and as enemies. They sit apart at meals; they sleep apart, and as a nation they are singularly prone to lust—though they refrain from intercourse with foreign women. Among themselves nothing is unlawful. Circumcision was adopted by them as a mark of their difference from other men" (*Hist.* 5).

The same writer, commenting on the great fire of Rome (64 C.E.) which Nero attributed to the Christians, paints the following picture: "Nero fabricated scapegoats [for the fire] and punished with every refinement the notoriously depraved Christians (as they were popularly called). Their originator, Christ, had been executed in Tiberius' reign by the governor of Judah, Pontius Pilate. But in spite of this temporary setback the deadly superstition had broken out afresh, not only in Judah but even in Rome. All degraded and shameful practices collect and flourish in the capital" (*Annals* 15.43).

For Tacitus, both Judaism and Christianity were "depraved" and immoderate: the charge of sexual immoderation would soon be transferred wholesale from Judaism to Christianity. Both were "degraded" and un-Roman in their exclusivism, which was tied to no national cult and was, therefore, unpatriotic from the standpoint of late Hellenistic understandings of religion as a set of beliefs that tie (*ligare/religare*) a nation together. It could be (and was) argued that Judaism had known a time when religion served precisely that function in subservience to the state cults of Rome. But that time had come and gone. Christianity, on the other hand, despite its protestations that it was the evolved form of Judaism, had never known the bond of religion and national identity. From the standpoint of Judaism, Christianity was *minuth*, apostasy. From the standpoint of Roman intellectuals, it was *superstitio*, religious enthusiasm, without historical credentials, or atheism because it seemed to worship "a man who has recently appeared" (thus Celsus [*Contra Celsum* 1.26]) as a god, without any relationship to the God worshiped by the Jews. Or (like Judaism) it was "hatred of mankind" (cf. Tertullian, *Apology* 37) for its refusal to do as the Romans did in matters religious.

Eventually Christianity found its counterblast in the belief that Christians were a "third race" and that the bond between particular nations and gods had been broken by the Christian doctrine of one God who watches over and deserves the allegiance of all nations (Tertullian, *Apology* 25). Occasionally, as from the mouths of Latin writers like Tertullian, bravado in the face of persecution could sound sedititious and threatening and was regarded as such by conservative intellectuals such as Celsus: "On valid grounds," writes Tertullian, "I might say that Caesar is more ours than yours, for our God has appointed him. . . . [Yet] let it suffice him to bear the name of emperor. That, too, is a great name of God's giving. To call him a god is to rob him of his title. If he is not a man, emperor he cannot be" (*Apology* 33).

text attributed to James sees the beginning of persecution as a test of Christian endurance, but acknowledges that patience is required in the face of overwhelming disappointment and insult to the new faith (James 5.7-11). The attribution of the letter to James, the brother of Jesus and caliph of the Jerusalem church after the crucifixion, makes it difficult to know what direction the abuse was coming from, though the "style" of the letter would make encounters between Christian believers and Jews outside Palestine a likely source for the writer's counsel. At around the same time (ca. 110) a letter attributed to an aged Peter some two generations after his death comments on an increase of "scoffers"—presumably Jewish and pagan writers who see the delay of the last days and Jesus' return as proof that Christians preached lies and practiced deceit: "We have not followed cunningly devised fables," the writer argues in defense of the churches (2 Peter 1.16), but acknowledges that his arguments are lost on "libertines" who have turned aside from the faith at the urging of skeptics (2.21). What the skeptics taught is made clear: "Where now [they ask] is the promise of [Jesus'] return? Because since the first believers fell asleep everything remains just as it was at the beginning of creation; nothing has changed" (2 Peter 3.4). While "Peter's" advice remained typical of Christian apologetic responses for a century thereafter—those who have disbelieved have misunderstood the prophecies—the attack on Christian apocalyptic rhetoric remains a feature of anti-Christian polemic until the fourth century and features prominently in Porphyry's assault.

CHRISTIAN MORALITY

The first generation of Christians died away without having experienced the fulfillment of their hopes. The manipulation of apocalyptic imagery and "forecasting," or the belief that unfulfilled prophecies had been misread prophecies, provided some consolation to the beleaguered community. Of more consequence, however, was a change in the perception of the risen-but-absent Jesus' relationship to the community. The soon-to-return Lord had always been understood to be—in some

sense—mystically (Matt. 28.20) as well as spiritually (John
20.22) and sacramentally (1 Cor. 11.26) present in the waiting
church. With the collapse of the eschatological hope for the
speedy return of Jesus the spiritual and sacramental presence
of Jesus was all that remained.

There is some evidence that certain churches of the Christian diaspora, despite efforts by Jewish missionaries like Paul
to curb their excesses, were ecstatic cults, that is, congregations which understood emotional, physical and sexual energy
as proofs of the presence of Christ within their community.
At Corinth, Paul complains that the community there exhibits
"such immorality as is not even found among the pagan." The
source of the trouble seems to have been a natural affinity
between the sacramental understanding of Christ as a god made
spiritually present through the outpouring of divine gifts
(*charismata*) and the ancestral rituals of the Corinthians themselves, which tended to be luxurious and highly emotional.
Paul's major themes in the letter are a configuration of the
problems that would define a church poised on the brink of
religious enthusiasm: celibacy versus marriage; incest; gluttony
associated with the eucharist; food-offerings to idols; spiritual
ecstacy, especially *glossolalia* or speaking in tongues; and the
mystery of resurrection of the body—the last of which the
Corinthians found either puzzling or unacceptable.

Paul's task at Corinth was to domesticate religious enthusiasm without losing the congregation in the process; to
make a distinction, in other words, between the "freedom" he
thought Christ had made available and the licentiousness that
seemed to follow from it. Christians who had never known
the constraints of Jewish law, however, would have had difficulty making sense of Paul's idea of freedom.

There is no specific evidence that the Christian church
in Corinth practiced *omophagia*, the tearing apart of a sacrificial victim and eating its warm flesh as the theriomorphic deity,
though Paul's use of body imagery in his first letter to the
Corinthians and the theme of spiritual communion through
incorporation into the "body of Christ" (1 Cor. 12.27f.) is familiar
from the language of the Dionysiac mysteries: "Blessed is he
who hallows his life in the worship of God, he whom the spirit

of God possesseth, who is one with those who belong to the holy body of God" (Euripides, *Bacchae* 73–75). Pagan critics of the early movement pointed to the fact that Christians addressed Jesus in terms equivalent to those used by the bacchantes (Dionysus' worshipers). Jesus was *kyrios* (lord) and *lysios*, redeemer. In the Dionysiac cult, the god redeemed adherents from a world of darkness and death by revealing himself in ecstatic visions and providing glimpses of a world-to-come.

The imagery of wine, already a feature of Christian worship having evolved from Passover ritual, was also a natural symbol in the context of bacchantic worship: immortality flowed from the god as wine flowed naturally from the grape, its red hue symbolizing the essence of life itself. In the Christian mystery, which incorporated the Dionysian wine ritual in the story of the wine miracle at Cana (John 2.11), the wine-element of the eucharist was understood both in terms of its Jewish association (i.e., the blood of the atoning, sacrificial victim: Rom. 5.6–11) and in Hellenic style (the blood of communion which imparts immortality to the believer: Ignatius, *To the Ephesians* 20.2). At Corinth, the excesses would suggest that the communion feasts were not merely drunken revels but specifically related to the sacramental understanding of the "gifts" made available through Jesus the Lord.

It is sometimes suggested that the pagan observers merely "misunderstood" Christian language, charged as it was with references to the "body and blood of the Lord" (cf. Tertullian, *Apology* 9) This observation, however, misses the point that the Christian churches in Macedonia and Rome were working out of a specific cultic context in which communion with the provisioning god was essential in the process of achieving immortality. As late as 170, Justin the Martyr, a Syrian writer, describes the eucharist "not as common bread and common drink [wine] to be received, but as food which is blessed by the prayer of his word and from which our blood and flesh by transmutation are nourished."

The problem of emotional and sexual excess linked to the sacramental understanding of Christ's presence was not limited to Corinth. At the beginning of the second century, an epistle written in the name of the apostle Jude was composed to imprecate those "who walk in the way of Cain and abandon themselves to Balaam's error and perish in Korah's rebellion" (Jude 11). The writer is especially severe against those Christians who "concern themselves with the things of the flesh and thus corrupt themselves" (Jude 10). The location of their excesses is said to be the Christian "love feasts" associated with, if not identical to, the eucharist (Jude 12); and their specific sins seem to include the flouting of rules designed to keep the love feasts sexually above board (Jude 8).

While the parochial history of the early church has tended to credit Tertullian's early third-century protestations of Christian innocence, it must be said that the early *second*-century church—the source of most later pagan assessments of Christianity—was an odd assortment of puritanical and enthusiastic congregations. For writers like Paul, the appropriate apocalyptic position toward the things of the flesh was denial (Rom. 6.12–15; 1 Cor. 6.10–19). God's judgment was to be pronounced on a world already deemed to be corrupt. To participate in a material way in its corruption was a mark of not having "received" the forgiveness made possible in Jesus Christ. Yet Paul could be interpreted antinominally—that is, as someone who taught the *permissibility* of all actions to those who knew themselves saved, and beyond the law. Indeed, the Christians at Corinth seem to have interpreted Paul in just this way. The enthusiasm for salvation was easily translated into a frenzy of the saved.

ROMAN OBSERVANCES AND ROMAN OBSERVERS

Fronto

The ritual practices of the Christians were certainly well known by the year 111, when the Roman governor of Bythynia, the younger Pliny, received reports of Christian excesses in his province. Professing a healthy skepticism about their practices and an ignorance of their belief, Pliny reports in his letter to the emperor Trajan that "[the Christians] claim to partake of food , but food of an ordinary and innocent kind." The charge,

later repeated by pagan critics of the cult, was either cannibalism or omophagia. In the same period, the Latin rhetorician
Marcus Cornelius Fronto (100–166) describes the rites of a sect
of Christians as abominations and affronts to the Roman sense
of decency:

> A young baby is covered over with flour, the object being
> to deceive the unwary. It is then served to the person to
> be admitted to the rites. The recruit is urged to inflict blows
> upon it which appear to be harmless because of the covering
> of flour. Thus the baby is killed with wounds that remain
> unseen and concealed. It is the blood of the infant—I shudder
> to mention it—it is this blood that they lick with thirsty
> lips; the limbs they distribute eagerly; this is the victim by
> which they seal the covenant. (Fronto, para. by Minucius
> Felix, *Octavius* 9.5–6)

Graphic as this description is, and marginal though the
group being described may be, it is doubtful that Fronto knew
what he was talking about. References in early Christian
writers to Jesus as the "lamb of God" and often the "child
of God," together with the sacrificial symbolism of the eucharist
and literal representations of the drinking of the blood of the
lamb, were enough to fuel Latin rhetoric of Fronto's variety.
He goes on to describe the incestuous passions of the sect
following their ritual communion:

> On a special day they gather in a feast with all their children,
> sisters, mothers, all sexes and ages. There, flushed with the
> banquet after such feasting and drinking, they begin to burn
> with incestuous passions. They provoke a dog tied to a
> lampstand to leap and bound toward a scrap of food, which
> they have tossed outside the reach of his chain. By this means
> the lamp is overturned and extinguished and with it common
> knowledge of their actions; in the shameless dark and with
> unspeakable lust they copulate in random unions, all being
> equally guilty of incest—some by deed but everyone by
> complicity. (*Octavius* 9.5–6)

In evaluating Fronto's attack, it is important to distinguish his viewpoint from that of critics such as Celsus and Porphyry. In the first place, Fronto was the tutor of Marcus Aurelius and his adopted brother, Lucius Verus. An African and a lawyer, Fronto seems to represent the views of the imperial court rather than those of the philosophical observer: slander and gossip are his stock and trade. Accordingly, the Christians are a rabble of ignorant fanatics and debauched conspirators who follow a man who was deservedly crucified. Fronto pays lip service to the gods of Rome, who have the greatness of Rome to commend them as objects of service and ritual devotion. The Christians have no such god. Their doctrines are absurd: They worship the head of an ass and believe that their god races about the world searching the hearts of humankind before destroying the world by fire and raising stinking corpses from their graves (cf. Tertullian, *Apology* 7). What we know of Fronto's attack is preserved in the speeches of Caecilius, the "agnostic" in Minucius Felix's dialogue, *The Octavius*. The charge of ass-worship is as old as Tacitus (*Hist.* 5.3.4), who alleges it of the Jews, and was known also to Posidonius, Apollonius Molon, and Apion.

Aristides

A more studious line of attack came from "religious" critics such as Aristides, another tutor of Marcus Aurelius and a devotee of the cult of the healer-god Asklepios. In his attack on the philosophy of the Cynics (*Oration* 46.2), Aristides compares them to the "impious men of Palestine who do not respect their betters." Like the Cynics, the Christian teachers are enemies of Greek culture, ridicule the philosophers, cause strife in households, do not see fit to attend the religious festivals and refuse any form of civic duty. Unlike the agnostic Fronto (as recorded in Caecilius), Aristides sees the Christians as shirking their religious obligations. They do not "conform" to old and established ways and cannot be taught true religion. The title of Celsus' attack on the Christians' *alēthēs logos*, or "true doctrine," suggests how sorely Christian obstinance and refusal to take lessons from the consensus of religious wisdom vexed the pagan teachers. The charge that Christians, like the Cynics, cause "strife in households which they cannot cure" is an interesting comment on the effect of the Christian mission on families. There is no doubt that families were torn apart over the preaching of the "Galileans" (as Epictetus referred to them). For their part, however, Christians ponted to Jesus' prophecy that families would fall to ruin over the gospel (Mark 13.12) and could then use this state of affairs as a sign that the last days were approaching.

Marcus Aurelius

The "persecuting" reign of Marcus Aurelius in the late second century (161–180) was driven by the emperor's religious convictions. More and more, Christian stubbornness and arrogance (obliviousness to their own error is the favorite way of construing it) come into play. To the Stoic emperor the Galileans appeared foolish. Their vaunted fearlessness in the face of death was not based (like Stoicism) on genuine philsophical principles but came to them out of habit, without appeal to reason or demonstration (*Discourses* 4.7.6) The criticism is not especially poignant. What the emperor meant to say was that Christians faced death obstinantly on the basis of irrational ideas, e.g., the belief in the resurrection of the body and the eternal life to come. Their courage was akin to childish ignorance and madness, and lacked the element of authentic acceptance with which a philosopher would greet the inevitability of his death or choose suicide (for example) over shame (cf. *Meditations* 11.3).

Galen

Writing in Rome around 170, the physician-philosopher Galen blamed the Christians for their invincible prejudice. While he admitted that their mode of teaching (parables) was decidedly inferior to philosophical demonstration, he speculated about their conduct, which seemed to him better than the base morality of others of their class. "We ought to beware of medical dogmatism lest, like those who have entered the school of Moses and Christ, we should start by lending our ears to laws that do not admit of demonstration" (*On the Usefulness of Body Parts* 2.4; 3.3). Yet, "It is easier to convert the followers of Moses and of Christ than physicians and philosophers, who have surrendered themselves to the scientific sects."

Contrary to what is sometimes suggested, Galen did not admire Christians for the outcome of their nonphilosophical approach to virtue. He agreed with Marcus Aurelius that the effect of their efforts, while agreeing with philosophically considered approaches, were based on ignorance and not on a desire for the truth. "In our time," he wrote, "we see those who are called Christians gathering their faith from parables. And yet sometimes they do just what the philosophers do. That they despise death is evident; we can see it with our own eyes. We also can see that they avoid sexual promiscuity: there are men and women in the Christian sect who remain celibate throughout their lives." The purity of this passage has often been challenged; Gregory Abulpharagius cited it in his *History of Dynasties* (1663) as coming from Galen's commentary on Plato's *Phaedo*. The argument for the partial authenticity of the passage stems from its observation that Christians "visibly despise death"—one that flies in the face of the familiar apologetic view that the martyrs embraced death gladly as assurance of their eternal reward (cf. Tertullian, *Scorpiace* 12).

From Aristides, Fronto, Marcus Aurelius and Galen we can construct what may be called the "moral" critique of Christianity. Christian worship, though in a transitional stage at the end of the second century, ranged in practice from ascetic to enthusiastic. Some sects, such as the Corinthians and Carpocratians, indulged in luxurious rites marked by drinking bouts and—perhaps—sexual license. Groups such as the Marcosians, known to the church writer Irenaeus and branded by him as heretical, seem to have practiced ritual prostitution in the Hellenistic style, and other groups, such as the Phibionites, took seriously the words ascribed to Jesus (Mark 16.18) concerning immunity from poison. The tendency to judge all Christians by the actions of these sectarian movements prompts

Justin Martyr to write before the end of the second century, "We demand that those accused to you be judged in order that each one who is convicted may be punished as an evildoer and not as a Christian" (1 *Apology* 7). By Tertullian's day (144–220), however, suspicion of the cult had increased and had become a favorite topic for literary invective. "Not one hundred and fifty years have passed since our life began," Tertullian writes (*To the Nations* 7f.); "yet the rumors that circulate against us, anchored in the cruelty of the human mind, enjoy considerable success. . . . If the Tiber has overflowed its banks, or if the Nile has remained in its bed, if the sky has been still or the earth has been disrupted, if plague has killed or famine struck, your cry is, 'Let the Christians have it!' " Among the charges that most worry Tertullian are those of cannibalism, murder, treason, sacrilege, and incest, and the general complaint that Christian clannishness prevents them from leading the lives of ordinary citizens: they avoid the clubs, religious associations, the theater and (though there were exceptions) military service.

Lucian

According to the early critics Tacitus, Pliny and Aristides, Christianity was to be judged according to the unwillingness of its adherents to compromise. They were superstitious fanatics given to outpourings of enthusiasm, or they occasionally indulged in sexual orgies in assocation with their eucharistic banquets.

With the satires of Lucian, the moral critique of the church enters a new phase. Born at Samosata (Syria) around 120, Lucian regarded Christianity as a form of sophistry aimed at an unusually gullible class of people—a criticism later exploited by Celsus (*Contra Celsum* 3.44). The members of the new sect worship a "crucified sophist," an epithet that suggests the influence of Jewish views of the church on pagan observers. Like Galen, Lucian imagines the Christians as men and women with little time, patience or ability for philosophy, and who are willing to enthrone new leaders and gurus at the drop of a hat. To make his point, Lucian invents a mock Cynicturned-Christian priest, Peregrinus Proteus, who dabbles in a thousand different sects and philosophies before becoming an "expert" in "the astonishing religion of Christianity." As a man of atypical abilities in the context of the new faith, Peregrinus rises quickly in the ranks:

> In no time at all he had them looking like babies and had become their prophet, leader, head of their synagogue and what-not all by himself. He expounded and commented on their sacred writings and even authored a few himself. They looked up to him as a god, made him their lawgiver, and put his name down as the official patron of the sect, or at least vice patron, second to that man they still worship today, the one who was crucified in Palestine because he brought this new cult into being. (*Death of Peregrinus* 10–13)

Lucian's "hero" is a shyster—the first example in literature of an anything-for-profit evangelist who bilks his congregations. The communal spirit and puling generosity of the Christian community are themes of Lucian's satire, as when a deputation of Christians from the cities of Asia come to Peregrinus' aid after he is arrested for treason: "And thus Peregrinus reaped a large harvest of money to console him in his bonds" (*Death* 13), "for their first lawgiver persuaded them that they are all brethren." To his dismay, the governor of Syria, a philosopher, sets Peregrinus free when he discovers the priest only wants to be a martyr. After he is refused the glory of martyrdom Peregrinus' enthusiasm for the new faith cools, "until one day . . . when the brethren saw him eating forbidden food and turned him out" (*Death* 16).

For all its looseness of detail, Lucian's portrait of Peregrinus can be said to reflect a popular view of the Christians at the close of the second century. They are both generous and gullible, quick to be seduced by anyone professing to share their faith, overadmiring of "true" philosophical talent, characteristically amiable but intolerant and suspicious, and bonded together (as Celsus would observe) out of fear rather than doctrinal agreement.

Celsus

The climax of late second-century critiques of Christianity comes in the work of the philosopher Celsus. Virtually nothing is known for certain of his life apart from what we learn from his eloquent and ardent opponent, Origen (185-254). According to spotty information, Celsus was active "during Hadrian's reign and later" (i.e., the thirties of the second century), though scholars have generally preferred to date him in the last quarter of the second century, during the persecutions at Lyon and Vienne. Origen, for polemical motives, calls Celsus an Epicurean—a term of abuse often meant to suggest atheism. In fact, his philosophy is that of a conservative middle Platonist. He holds that the vulgar must have their parables and myths, but that philosophy is the only true guide to life. Like Plutarch, he argues that there is one supremely good God who employs a vast array of *daimones* (some good, some evil) who act as influences within the material world.

Against Judaism and Christianity, Celsus holds that man is not the foremost of God's creatures: "If a man kills a tiger, a tiger kills a man." Animals exceed humans in wisdom and social relations; elephants, storks and the phoenix are more pious while bees are more industrious, wise and sociable. Christianity and Judaism err, therefore, when they think that the nobility of humankind, as the "highest" of God's creation, would cause the divine being to undergo change, to show pity, or to involve himself in the rescue of a world governed adequately by his own ministering spirits.

Celsus' argument has been called the first thorough-going attack upon the whole Christian position. Celsus had studied the subject as no writer before him appears to have done, and it would wait until Porphyry at the end of the third century for someone as well versed in the gospels to produce a detailed refutation of Christian ideas. Celsus had read one or two of the gospels, Genesis, Exodus, and some of the Pauline epistles; had studied gnostic (and other peripheral) texts; and was aware of differences in Jewish and Christian interpretations of the prophets. Celsus was better acquainted than Origen with gnosticism, but sometimes conflates "Catholic" and "gnostic" Christian teaching in the course of his attack.

In his comments, Celsus attempts impartiality: He is no admirer of Judaism ("runaway Egyptian slaves who have never done anything worth mentioning") but acknowledges the antiquity of Jewish teaching and juxtaposes it with the newness of Christian doctrine. He thinks Christian teachers are no better than the begging priests of Cybele and the shysters of other popular religions. Importantly, Celsus does not dwell on the impurity of Christian ritual (though he alludes to it), but emphasizes that Christians are sorcerers like their founder, that they lack patriotism, and that every Christian church is an illegal association which exists not because their God arranges it (thus Tertullian), but because the emperor does not choose to stamp them out entirely.

The *True Word* or *True Doctrine* of Celsus was divided into two sections. In the first, Celsus presents a Jew as the antagonist to Christianity; in the second, he argues his own case. The strategy seems intended to show that Christianity is opposed not only by the philosophers of the "pagan" empire, but also by those with whom Christianity claims to have the closest affinity. In this way, the church could be seen to have neither the wisdom of the philosophical schools nor the antiquity of custom and law to its credit. Its teaching was merely eccentric—sectarian in the mean sense of the word. In his hierarchy of civilization, the Egyptians were beast-worshipers, the Jews infinitely worse in their religious practices, and the Christians renegade Jews "whom their miserable countrymen despised and hated." What would have aroused official distaste for Christanity, however, was Celsus' suggestion that the Christians were "breaking the religious peace of the world." With an outlaw as their head, they were rebels by nature and tradition.

Celsus' "Jew" is strident in his dialogue with the Christian teacher on the failure of the life of Jesus, a theme to which Poprhyry will return over a century later. That Celsus would emphasize this theme is unsurprising: we have already noted that it was at the heart of the earliest Jewish-Christian "dialogue" and their fictional reenactments by teachers like Justin. Celsus' "Jew" is, however, a more worthy opponent than Justin's. In the pagan dialogue, the Jew lectures the Christian; in Justin's the Christian lectures—and defeats—the Jew.

Familiar slanders resurface in the *True Doctrine*: Jesus was the son of a woman named Mary by a Roman soldier named Panthera. The prophets foretold a great king, a ruler and leader of armies—not an inconspicuous criminal who could not even command the loyalty of his disciples. There was no proof of his power: Pentheus was torn to shreds for imprisoning the god Bacchus, but Pontius Pilate suffered nothing in reprisal for crucifying Jesus. Why did he refuse to save himself and to punish those who had betrayed him? Celsus' "Jew" continues:

> The truth is, as long as he [Jesus] lived he persuaded nobody, not even his own disciples, and finally was punished and endured all this. His life here was a complete failure—and yet you want to argue that having failed to persuade people here, he marched down to Hell to persuade people there. You invent absurd excuses for him, but if we are to accept them [we will need to know] why we should accept anyone who has been condemned and died a miserable death as a divine messenger? Anyone who is rash enough may say of a robber, "This was no robber but a god, for he foretold his fellow robbers what he was to suffer."

As to the miracles, Celsus rejects them on the premise that Jesus himself acknowleged that even wicked men could work miracles (Mark 3.25). Prophecies of the Christ's suffering and death are rejected both because they do not seem to refer to the fate of Jesus specifically and because, if true, they would have caused Jesus to face his death with Stoic courage and resignation. The resurrection is rejected on the grounds that the only witnesses were "women half crazy from fear and grief, and possibly one other from the same band of charlatans, who dreamed it all up or saw what he wanted to see—or more likely, simply wanted to astonish his friends with a good tale."

As a Platonist Celsus believed in the immortality of the soul and the unchangeabilty of the divine being. The derivatives of this belief led to a "steady state" theory of creation, which denied any positive relationship between the divine being and the world. Among other conclusions, Celsus holds that because evil is inherent in matter there can never be more or less evil in the material world. Christian doctrine saw evil as having "entered" the world with the sin of Adam and increasing from age to age, until the time of the redeemer when its control weakened (Rom. 5.12–17). Similarly, Celsus' world needs no "improvements," no saviors. Revelation or an increase in revelation is contrary to the use of reason, and reason's systematic expression is philosophy. Thus, philosophy is the "true doctrine" of which all the best religious teachings are unsystematic, provisional, or preliminary expressions.

What irritates Celsus the most, however, is the impudence of Christian teachers with their stories about the incarnation and resurrection of Jesus. Insofar as these stories have any value, they are blundering attempts to repeat in a coarse fashion the stories of the ancient myths. The style of Christian preaching also comes under attack:

> They are forever saying, "Do not inquire, only believe. . . ." This is their cry: Let no educated men enter in, no one wise, no one prudent, for these things we count as evil. But if any be ignorant, any foolish, any untaught, anyone simple-minded, let him come boldly. These they count worthy (as indeed they are) of their god, and it is therefore obvious that they can and will persuade only fools and the lowborn, the dull-witted, slaves, foolish women, and little children [*Contra Celsum* 3.44]. . . . We see in private houses wool carders, cobblers, fullers, the most ignorant and stupid of characters who would never dare open their mouths in the hearing of their teachers and intellectual betters. [But these then] get the children and women into corners and tell them wonderful things. "Do not listen to your father or your teachers," they will say, "Listen to us! Your teachers don't know what we know; they're too full of learning and systems. We alone know how to live; listen to us and you will be healthy, happy and prosperous." (*Contra Celsum* 3.55)

Obliged to operate among the "misfits" of Roman society, as Celsus thought of them, the Christians had made a virtue of necessity, insisting that the kingdom of god was for the unrighteous and not the virtuous. His comments on the social and moral situation of converts to the new faith serve almost as an epitome of anti-Christian polemical writing:

The priests of the other mystery [cults] cry, "Come, you who
are clean of heart, discreet of tongue and pure of sin, those
whose life has been good and just and free from deceit." But
whom do the Christians invite? The sinners. The foolish. The
childish. The unhappy. These the kingdom of God will admit.
The sinner! The unjust, the thief, the burglar, the prisoner,
the robber of temples and tombs. [This preaching] is a robber's
invitation. God [is] sent to sinners—not to the sinless. What
harm is there in being without sin? The unjust man brought
down by his wickedness, God will receive; but the just man
who practices virtue and looks up to God from the beginning,
that man God will not receive. The wardens of prisons order
the prisoners to stop their wailing before the judge, so that
justice can be administered fairly and not out of pity. The
Christian God, however, is guided in his judgments not by
truth but by flattery. (*Contra Celsum* 3.59, 62-3)

Celsus intensely disliked everything about Christians and
their teaching. He is not even willing to grant—as Galen evidently was—that their actions are naively virtuous even though
their philosophy is contemptible. With Fronto and Marcus
Aurelius, he argues that their defenselessness, the fact that
they stand condemned solely on the basis of the faith they
profess, is proof enough that their God has no power to save
them. Celsus thought that extreme measures were the right
way to deal with fanaticism. If the "martyrs" suffer, they suffer
out of sheer obstinacy, not (as they say) because their cause
is destined to prevail. The God professed by the Christians
seems to have deserted them—as he deserted the Jews before
them. As a religious "conservative" by Roman standards, a
man who undertands *pietas* essentially as loyalty to what the
state approves, Celsus finds the Christians ungrateful: should
Caesar fall, the control of the earth would fall into the hands
of uncultured, irreligious (= disloyal) and lawless barbarians,
and insofar as the Christians look for the end of the world
or the end of Roman hegemony over the world, lawlessness
must be what they want (*Contra Celsum* 8.69-75).

PORPHYRY AND HIS TIME

By 270 Christianity and traditional Roman religion were on a collision course. Fewer than fifty years later, Christianity would survive the encounter—changed, to be sure, but indisputably the healthiest of the cults recognized by the state. Military successes in the east around 272 were attributed by the emperor Aurelian to the sun god at Emesa, and in the final years of his reign Aurelian installed the god (*Sol Invictus*) as the Lord of the empire, built a temple in his honor, struck coins bearing the image of the emperor receiving the orb of majesty from Jupiter directly, and created a new class of senator-priests devoted to his worship.

The image of the "unconquerable sun" was thereafter etched in the religious consciousness. Constantine was reported by the church historians Eusebius and Lactantius as receiving a vision of the cross (The "crossed" Greek letters *chi* [X] and *rho* [P]) imposed on the disc of the sun at the battle of the Mulvian Bridge in 312. As described by Eusebius (*Life of Constantine* 1.28), the emperor-to-be had read the words "*in hoc [signo] vinces* (In this sign you shall conquer)," the sign being that of the Christian cross. Like Aurelian before him, Constantine attributed the augur to the divine being—in this case a synthesis of the Sol Invictus and the Christian God. His correspondence suggests that he was not terribly concerned to make the distinction (his coins professed his allegiance to the sun god), though he did not reopen persecution of the Christians and was thus remembered as their liberator. The power and persistence of the symbol, however, could be shown by the fact that in 325, still during Constantine's reign, Christian bishops in Nicaea would define the power of Christ and his relation to God the father as "light from [the] light, true God from true God." More graphically, the early (ca. 300?) mosaic known as "Christos Helios" ("Christ the Sun") in the mausoleum under St. Peter's in Rome shows a glorified Christ having assimilated the attributes of the sun god. He holds a globe in his left hand and drives a chariot pulled by a team of horses, like Apollo. Grape vines surround the central figure—an allusion to the life-giving wine of Dionysus, but also to Christ, the true vine, whose "life" is made available in the eucharist.

To return for the moment to Aurelian: the emperor was pressed at the end of his reign to launch an attack against the Christians and to make the religion of the sun god universal in the empire. Ostensibly, this was a period of renewed self-confidence in Rome and its institutions. The coins of the Illyrian soldier-emperor, Probus (276–282), proclaim the age of an "eternal Rome and her companion, the unconquerable sun." The help of the gods was invoked as seldom before to ensure a new Augustan age of security and peace.

This security was guaranteed in part by the military successes of the emperor, but "eternal Rome" needed philosophical defending as well. This came in the form of two pupils of the neoplatonic philosopher Plotinus: Porphyry of Tyre (d. 304) and Amelius (fl. 246–270), the "senior boy" in Porphyry's school. Neoplatonism had already emerged as a nexus between Christianity and paganism in the work of Origen of Alexandria against Celsus' *True Doctrine*. The two "systems" had beliefs in common. They blended philosophical principles with religious ideals, believed in a universe guided by the influence of a providential being (and his subordinate gods and demigods, in the case of the pagan philosophers), and acknowledged equally the possibility of divine union or mystical "ascent" to that providential being and the power of divine insight, "clairvoyance" or theurgy—god-given magical power that permitted the seer to speak with authority about things unseen. Christianity had been infused in one way or another with these ideas from two sides: in its battles with Platonizing gnosticism in the second and third centuries and in its ongoing struggle to develop a philosophical vocabulary suitable for its place and time. From Clement of Alexandria right through to Athanasius, the workshop for this vocabulary was the Christian "academy" of Alexandria with its amalgam of ideas borrowed from Plato, the Stoics, Pythagoras, and assorted minor philosophical systems and religious cults.

For all this agreement, however, differences between state-sponsored philosophy and the Christian theologians were substantial. The Christian tendency had always been—as its critics alleged—to reason from the "facts" of revelation and to employ philosophy as needed or when convenient. This meant that the use of philosophical reasoning was in the service of the sacred texts. There were those, of course, above all Origen, who spent long hours attempting to reconcile the meaning of revelation with the practice of philosophy. In the end, however, he fell between the stools, between the gnostics and Plotinus, in his attempts to rescue the Bible from its historical and literary limitations. The "plain sense" of the text was an embarrassment to the philosophically disposed Christian ("How can Christ have been lifted up to a mountain high enough to see all the kingdoms of the world: there is no such mountain?"). At such moments, Origen can sound almost like his pagan opponents. For him, however, the doctrine of inspiration immunizes the text against "real" self-contradiction and error. The Bible is an enormous allegory, a series of divine pardoxes, a book full of mysterious meanings. How else could the divine mystery be expressed, except in parables and signs that occasionally thwart commonsense interpretations? The Bible revealed its meaning to the Christian soul— also a great mystery—and this soul can be prepared for enlightenment by philosophy. Origen tried and failed to do for Christianity what the Platonists (including Porphyry) had done for Homer, namely, to turn a diverse literature into a species of religious truth. After his death, his efforts were condemned as heretical.

As a result of Origen's failure to provide a philosophical shield for the faith of the apostles, the quarrel between "Athens and Jerusalem," as Tertullian had styled the distinction between philosophy and Christian teaching, became increasingly vicious. To the Romans the Christian charge of idolatry as applied to their religion was as galling as the pagan charge of atheism was to the Christians. Claims of "Thyestean banquests," incest, and rampant immorality were hurled by each in the other direction, while the Christians were repeatedly blamed for their lack of *pietas*—loyalty to Rome and her ways— and their indifference to civic duty. Neoplatonic philosophers such as Amelius (ca. 270) criticized the gospels for their barbarian origins. And despite Eusebius' claims that Amelius teachers such as Justin, Origen and Minucius Felix had long since affected this style of literary opposition, though their opponents were either dead (Celsus) or fictionalized (Justin's Trypho), thus rendering them more amenable to persuasion. In taking on the Christians later in his career, Porphyry was issuing the same sort of challenge he had issued to Plotinus in 263. Unfortunately, there was no Christian Amelius to take him on, though a number tried: Eusebius, the church historian; Jerome; Methodius of Olympus; Apollinarius of Laodicaea; and Macarius Magnes did their best.

Porphyry joined a group that included pupils from all over the empire: Romans, Greeks, Arabs and Egyptians, and doubtless a number of Jews. Porphyry's encyclopaedic knowledge of the ways and customs of the world originates in discussion—informal and formal—with his fellow students. Plotinus himself lived frugally, in the ancient manner of the Peripatetics, living as a guest in the houses of friends whether in Rome or away on "tour." He died penniless, on the estate of an Arab named Zethas. During his life Plotinus lived "as one ashamed of his body," suffered from indigestion which seems to have been brought on by his vegetarian diet (cf. *Life* 9.2), and refused to speak about himself or his needs. Plotinus' style as a teacher was both systematic and unstructured: he began by explaining Plato, then Aristotle, then the divergences between them, regarding this explication as the "foundation course" in philosophy. He then moved on to discuss the Stoics, the Peripatetics, and the "moderns," presumably including the philosophy of the Christians, whom he knew as gnostics and termed "unreasonable":

> These [Christian] teachers in their contempt for this creation and this earth proclaim that another earth has been made for them into which they are to enter when they depart. Now this new earth [they think] is the the Logos of our world [the heavenly archetype]. Why should they want to live in the archetype of a world which is abhorrent to them? (2 Ennead 9.5; cf. *Apocriticus* II.12-15)

The doctrine of the beauty of this world and the unsoundness of Christian teaching in the area of metaphysics would become one of Porphyry's themes in *Against the Christians.*

The ethos of Plotinus' circle was actively anti-Christian, even though the teacher himself was indirect rather than polemical in his attack. He proposed problems based on a close reading of the relevant texts, raised incidental questions, and probed and prodded until he was satisfied that the meaning of the text—and its associated questions—was completely clear. From the standpoint of Socratic method, the Christian style was distinctly un-Socratic, consisting of injunctions to have faith and *believe* rather than ask questions. The Christian concept of truth consisted of revealed propositions in search of philosophical legitimation; it was doctrinaire where Platonism was dynamic.

Porphyry excelled in learning his teacher's method and was often singled out for praise. On May 7, the inner circle celebrated Plato's birthday as a red letter day in the form of a symposium—a drinking fest and banquet, which always included oratorical and song competetions. On at least one occasion, Porphyry won acclaim: for his philosophical poem, "Of the Heavenly Marriage," a hymn to the Platonic ideal of beauty reminiscent of the *Symposium.*

A word, at least, should be said to summarize Plotinus' teaching, as it has come down to us through Porphyry's transcription in the *Enneads.* From Plato, Plotinus derived the belief that all genuine knowledge is knowledge of the ideal form of a material thing. Philosophy rather than the mystery cults was the means to free oneself from the oppression of the material world—understood as a world of destruction, plague, war and famine, disease and death—but also a world in which truth shines through, where corruptible images point to the ideal archetypes. Like Plato, Plotinus believed that the human soul originated from above and contained within it certain "information" (powers) from the world of ideas. Submerged in the material world of becoming rather than "being," the soul is confused, tossed, handicapped by bodily existence (4 *Ennead* 1.8; 4.14). The soul must be taught to oppose the forces at was created as an expression of divine *nous*, i.e., mind or will. The constellations and heavenly bodies are "revelations" of the gods in their totality, like "books" that can be read to obtain information about them.

While superficially this "theology" sounds like the same Platonizing use of images as conveyances or shadows of an ultimate reality used in Christian circles, Porphyry's understanding of myth was essentially historical: myths were parables pf philosophical truth. In Christianity, the myth *was* the truth. According to the Porphyrian myth, the soul descends as an astral particle acquiring more and more mass as it descends through the universe. Even after death and the decay of the body, the soul is doomed to enter into new bodies which effectively make its ascent impossible. Religion offers a "theoretical" solution: it teaches that the body can be purified by means of magical practices—ablutions and baptisms—which are attempts to exorcize the demons or to win them over as friends, thereby arranging for the soul's partial ascent or escape from the powers that rule the world (cf. Paul, 2 Cor. 12.2-4). Belief in God as a pure intellectual principle and ground of virtue was recommended because it was a benefit for humans to aspire to the "divine mind": "You will best honor God by making your mind like unto him, and this you can do by virtue alone. For only virtue can draw the soul upward to that which is akin to it. Next to God there is nothing great but virtue" (*Letter to Marcella* 49).

While Porphyry's language can often sound "Christian"—an annoyance to Augustine, who concluded that the philosopher was always half right and thus all wrong—it is clear upon inspection that Porphyry found the Christians annoying on just the same terms. Porphyry tells us in language prefiguring Augustine that the soul in need of God is restless, but Porphyry (unlike the Christian bishop) reserves this longing for the wise man, since "God is best honored by him who knows him best. And this must naturally be the wise man alone, who in wisdom must honor the divine, and in wisdom adorn for it a temple in his thought" (*Marcella* 46). Like Christian teachers from Tertullian onward, who taught that human sinfulness was an impediment to the knowledge of God (a clouding of the reason) and hence could be regarded as the condition which made revelation—a divine "overcoming" of the natural impediment—necessary for salvation, Porphyry saw sinfulness as the choice which fools made against virtue, and hence as what made them unwise. "To the wise man God gives the authority of a god and a man is purified by the knowledge of God. . . . But of evil, we ourselves are the authors" (*Marcella* 47).

Given the different analysis of the source of evil, Porphyry could find the Christian view of salvation only contemptible. It seemed to him to require nothing of humans and everything of a God who had been compromised by his own creation—put into the position of working out a clever trick to save human beings from their own natures. Though this is veiled or submerged in his letter to Marcella, Porphyry recognized that the linguistic similarity between his own teaching and that of the "Sophist" [Christian] teachers might confuse those who are looking for the God represented by the philosophers. Thus, he advises his wife, Marcella, not to associate with "anyone whose opinions cannot profit you, nor join with him in converse about God," since "it is not fitting for a man who is not purified from unholy deeds to speak about God" (*Marcella* 15). The Christian view that the son of God came to save the wicked and unrighteous was scandalous; godlike (virtuous) deeds should precede any discussion of God. The wise man is distinguished by his deeds; he does nothing unworthy of God, who does nothing contrary to virtue and holiness. Thus the pursuit of virtue is not only the trademark of the wise man's nature; it actually makes him godlike : "A man worthy of God is a god" (*Marcella* 15). Although certain Christian teachers, including Athanasius, could dub salvation the "godding" of the elect, the idea was conspicuously alien to the mainstream of Christian thought and tended to threaten the doctrines of divine sovereignty and humankind's reprobation. For Porphyry, becoming godlike was the active quest of every soul that loved virtue and aspired to excellence. And it was precisely the Platonic doctrine of excellence that—from the philosopher's standpoint—Christianity lacked.

Porphyry's "God," therefore, has no need to save because he is not affected by sin. This is not to say that the philosopher fails to recognize a category of actions which are displeasing to God. But these actions are expressions of active failure and not of a passive genetic deficiency in a God-created race of men, as Augustine theorized. God strengthens those who practice virtue and "noble deeds" (*Marcella* 16), but he does not (cannot) punish those who fail to practice virtue or who do things contrary to virtue (*Marcella* 17), since the divine nature can only work for the good. Accordingly, the classical Christian theodicy does not arise in Porphyry's thought; he thinks it foolish to speculate, on Christian premises, about an all-good God, creator of an originally good world, over which, through lack of foresight (omniscience) or power (omnipotence) evil reigns and in which he is obliged to intervene time and time again. The puzzles of Christian theology are non-puzzles for Porphyry: The pieces comprise not a picture but a muddle, and can only be slotted together by trimming edges and omitting embarrassingly contorted segments. This, however, does not prevent Christian priests and teachers from selling their wares as a kind of philosophy. While religious observances—pagan or Christian—are not actually harmful, they encourage the simple-minded in a belief that God has need of them. The only true priests are the wise of the world, not the "fools praying and offering sacrifice." The only truly sinful man is "he who holds the opinions of the multitudes concerning God" (*Marcella* 17), and those who think that tears, prayers, and sacrifices can alter the divine purpose. The Christian God fails, in Porphyry's view, because he epitomizes false opinion, baseless hopes. He is changeable, fickle, unpredictable. His priests preach "mere unreasoning faith [in a God] who is gratified and won over by libations and sacrifices," without perceiving that men making exactly the same request receive different answers to their prayers (*Marcella* 23). Worse, human beings seem to believe that their basest actions can be erased by prayer, or, caught in the web of their own illogic, they become haters of the world and the flesh and mistakenly accuse the flesh of being the source of all evil (*Marcella* 29). "Salvation" for Porphyry cannot begin with self-hatred or the abnegation of the flesh. In its demythologized form, it is simply the "soul's" quest for wisdom as expressed in the pursuit of virtue—an acknowledgment of redemption being natural to the soul because of the soul's affinity to God. Porphyry does not think of the body as vile; he thinks of it as the discardable "outer man," whose satisfaction cannot be a final end or goal because it is corruptible, limited and earthbound. The body defines creaturely existence and not the soul's quest.

This description of Porphyry's philosophy, deriving chiefly from his letter to Marcella, a widow with seven children whom he married when he was almost seventy, is often seen as proof that Porphyry and the Christians shared certain religious values (Wilken, p. 134), as, for example, when he invokes the principles of faith, truth, hope and love as the appropriate ones concerning God (cf. 1 Cor. 13.13). The linguistic parallels, however, are misleading, especially if the trip undertaken "for the need of the Greeks" (*Marcella* 4), occurring around the time Diocletian was mounting a new assault against the Christian church, was actually undertaken to prepare a defense of traditional (Roman) religion against the Christians. That Porphyry was immersed in Christian books and Christian vocabulary in preparation for writing this defense would account for the style of the writing, as well as for its strategic difference from Christian teaching. The historian Lactantius mentions a "priest of philosophy living in Constantinople" who undertook to defend Roman religion and pejorate Christian teaching (*Divine Inst.* 5.2), though it is not certain that he means Porphyry.

AGAINST THE CHRISTIANS

The first thing to say about Porphyry's fifteen books against the Christians is that they are lost. The exact title is not known, and its popular title, *Kata Christianōn*, can be dated securely only from the Middle Ages. Opinions radically differ over the question whether the books can be substantially restored. A few facts can be stated succinctly, however. First, the church was unusually successful in its efforts to eradicate all traces of *Against the Christians* from at least 448. Not only were Porphyry's books destroyed, but many of the works of Christian

Christianity had no special interest in the antiquity of Judaism (though Porphyry may have thought that it did—since we have seen that the argument "from antiquity" was a key factor in earlier indictments of Christianity as a new religion. It did, however, have some interest in the Book of Daniel, which figured prominently in the gospels and in Christian apocalyptic thinking about Jesus as the son of man. On philological grounds, Porphyry seems to have argued that the book belonged to a later period and described the events of the authors' own time— the Maccabean period of the second century B.C.E.—rather than events that were still to unfold. (Jerome, *Comm. on Daniel*, prol.) The idea that the Book of Daniel was not prophetic was profoundly disturbing, provoking responses from Eusebius, Methodius, and St. Jerome, whose commentary on Daniel was a defense of the traditional Christian view.

That view, dominant since the second century, was that Daniel contained prophecies essential to establish certain elements of Christian belief. Both Justin the Martyr and Hippolytus argued that the chronology of Daniel accurately predicted the birth of the messiah, the destruction of the temple in Jerusalem, and the second coming. What Porphyry did was to undermine a whole system of Christian interpetation based on the prophetic value of the book (Wilken, p. 141). Elsewhere, Porphyry seems to have ridiculed the Book of Jonah (cited by Augustine, *Ep.* 102), which Christians had used as a prophecy of the resurrection (Matt. 12. 39–41; 16.4): "It is improbable and incredible that a man should have been swallowed up with his clothing on in the inside of a fish." The carping literalism with which the philosopher approached these questions, as recounted by Augustine, Jerome, and others, parallels closely the approach recorded in the work of Macarius Magnes, where allegory is systematically rejected as a means of avoiding inconsistencies or improbabilities in the biblical accounts.

Porphyry had perfected this technique of narrative criticism in his early work on Homer. Unreserved in the comprehensiveness of his treatment, Porphyry did not stop at the conclusion that the Book of Daniel was written four centuries later than Jews and Christian taught. He insisted, according to St. Jerome, that the prophetic interpretation was inconsistent even with the claims Christians made for the book: The Christians seemed to say that the Book of Daniel was—so to speak—doubly prophetic: if written before the Captivity in the sixth century, it pointed forward to events of the second century (namely, the Syrian violation of the temple precinct in 167 B.C.E.) *as well as* to events which took place under the Romans after the time of Christ—the burning of the temple. Christian teachers claimed that Jesus himself had invoked the prophecy in forecasting the destruction of the temple (Mark 13.2). But if the book was written about events in its own time—namely the second century—then it had no prophetic value at all. The Christians were mistaken. And if Jesus had cited it, then Jesus was mistaken as well.

It is impossible to know whether there is a specific cause, other than an intellectual's impatience with error, for Porphyry's assault. A number of scholars continue to maintain (*contra* Barnes) that he was deeply troubled by the spread of Christianity (Frend, *Rise*, p. 587), though some—Fox and Demarolle among them—question the passages that had supported this view (Fox, *Pagans*, p. 586). On average, the skepticism seems unwarranted. The famous statement cited by Macarius Magnes, that Porphyry complained of how the "Christians were building up great houses where they could assemble for prayer, [with] no one preventing them from doing this" (*Apocriticus* 4.21 and Harnack, *Gegen die Christen*, frag. 76, p. 93) is entirely consistent with the views of a depressed observer of events at the end of the late third century C.E.— a man who, like Swinburne's "Julian the Apostate," grimaces at the passing of the old order, the victory of the Galileans, the staleness of their teaching. Furthermore, we know from Augustine (*City of God* 19.23) that Porphyry complained of the influx of educated women into the church; in his *Philosophy from Oracles*, written around 263, he laments (*en masque* as Apollo, the god of enlightenment) that it is almost impossible to win back anyone who has converted to Christianity: it is easier, he says, to write words on water than try to use argument on a Christian. They simply cannot understand the folly of worshiping as a god a man who had died as a criminal. Despite the persecutions, Lactantius tells us, Christians

THE ERA OF ANTI-CHRISTIAN FEELING

It is difficult to say when Christians were singled out for special opprobrium by the Romans. Anti-Semitism had been centuries in the making and had passed as an inherited set of attitudes to the Romans from the common lore of the Hellenistic world. The Jews were "difficult, stiffnecked, religiously uncompromising." Yet their laws were acknowledged to be old, if eccentric, and their historical scholarship impressive.

On the other hand, Christianity's claim to have "completed" the law, while not an outright rejection of Judaism's claim to antiquity, was at least a rejection of antiquity's ability to serve as a means of testing the truth of a religious system. Furthermore, the apocalyptic vision of history prevented Christians from engaging in serious reflection on their historical situation: they stood "at the end of time" with their eyes turned heavenward for the coming of their savior. Only as this vision waned did they develop a historical "consciousness" of the world and their chronological location within it.

The attack on Christian belief in the resurrection and on the messianic teaching of the Christians, which included their interpretation of prophecy, had originated in the synagogue (cf. 2 Cor. 11.22–25). When Christian hopes for the speedy return of Jesus as the Son of Man did not materialize, a new target of criticism presented itself, one that was utilized first by Jewish opponents to show the incompetence of Christian scriptural interpretation, and then by pagan critics of the new religion. Christian defenses of their belief in the coming of the savior were already circulating in oral form before the fifties of the first century. Paul is aware of a movement in the church in Thessalonike to abandon or radically alter the new faith, apparently at the instigation of Jewish preachers, who come in for some unusually harsh criticism from Paul or his secretary (1 Thess. 2.12–15). In his letter to the Christians at Thessalonike, Paul claims to have been "driven away" by Jewish interlopers who have planted doubts in the mind of the Macedonian Christian churches about the "promise" of Christ's return (1 Thess. 4.15f.). As the mission progressed with its apocalyptic teaching persistently an issue in debates with itinerant Jewish teachers, the churches developed a variety of strategies for dealing with the delay:

- the gentiles would be converted before the last days (Mark 13.10)
- the power of pagan Rome and of the emperor would decline before God's son could be revealed in glory (Rom. 16.20; 2 Thess. 2.2–10)
- Jesus himself had professed ignorance about the time of this coming (Mark 13.32), or had refused to speculate about the signs of the last days (Mark 8.11–12)
- the kingdom of God was already working "secretly" and was being progressively realized through the success of the Christian mission (Luke 12.49–56; 17.22–37; Matt. 38–42).

It is best to regard these rationales as defensive and experimental. Jewish apocalyptic tradition itself had been mystically vague, studiously mysterious with respect both to the "timing" of the apocalyptic events and to the identity of the son of man. Christianity did not so much invent its imprecision as use it to advantage, having mimicked the style of its Jewish prototype (cf. 4 Esdras 5.1–8; Matt. 24.15–31, etc.). The fact that the destruction of the temple in 70 C.E. was factored into this imagery at around the time the gospels were being transcribed (cf. Mark 13.14–15; Luke 21.20) suggests that many Christians associated the end of the temple cult with the imminent return of Jesus. A flimsy tradition suggests that the Jerusalem Christians fled from the city before Titus' final assault to await the coming of Jesus in Pella (Khirbet Fahil) in the Decapolis. But a competing tradition (which the Christians currying Roman favor would have wanted to mute) linked the killing of James "the Lord's brother" to the siege on Jerusalem and the destruction of the temple (Josephus, according to Origen, *Contra Celsum* 1.47 and 2.13; *Comm. on Matthew* 10.17). If the "Josephus" tradition is accurate, then the Christians withdrew from Jerusalem following the failure of apocalyptic signs to materialize after the burning of the temple.

Their disappointment is registered in a variety of late New Testament writings. A very late first or early second-century found much to praise in the Christian *logos* doctrine (John 1.1-18) he seems primarily to have regarded the Christian doctrine as a theft from Stoic teaching.

THE LIFE OF PORPHYRY

Amelius was succeeded as a watchdog of the Christian movement by someone known even by Augustine as the ablest philosopher of them all—Porphyry of Tyre in Hellenized Phoenicia, whose name was originally Malkos.

Accounts of Porphyry's origins are notoriously confused— owing largely to Christian traditions concerning his life. Two fifth-century writers and a notable early twentieth-century historian (Harnack) believed he had been a Christian. The conclusion depends on our reading his anti-Christian polemic as a case of "lapsed Catholicism," a sellout to court philosophy, and as the best way of accounting for his mastery of Jewish and Christian sources. Church fathers from Eusebius to Augustine were intimidated by Porphyry's challenges and arguments—so much so that his worthiest opponent (Macarius Magnes) is not an especially articulate one, wholly unable to play the role of Origen to his Celsus. Constantine in the fourth century and Theodosius in the fifth decided that the only way to overcome Porphyry's objections was to put his books to the torch. Thus, the extent of his writings against Christianity is unknown. What we know (see the following bibliography) must be gleaned from a scattering of references, quotations and paraphrases in the writings of an army of church writers from the fourth century onward.

Whatever Porphyry's origins—his biographer, Eunnapius, locates his birth in Tyre in 233—Porphyry visited Palestine, Syria and Alexandria in his youth. His knowledge of the geography of the region permits him to challenge the description of certain scenes in the gospels—for example, the story of the Gadarene demoniacs—with which the evangelists themselves had only a scanty acquaintance. By the time of the persecutions of Christians under the emperor Decius (ca. 250), Porphyry was a committed enemy of the young religion. Eusebius tells us that Porphyry heard the lectures of Origen in Caesarea and was profoundly disappointed with the famous Christian philosopher's attempts to reconcile Platonic principles with Christian doctrine: "A Greek educated in Greek [Origen] plunged headlong into barbarian recklessness. Immersed in this, he peddled himself and his skill in argument. In this way of life he behaved like a Christian . . . [but] in his metaphysical and theological ideas he played the Greek, giving a Greek twist to foreign tales" (Eusebius, *Eccles. History* 6.19).

Porphyry studied philosophy with Longinus at Athens for six years. There, like many philosophical dillettantes before and since, he flirted with a variety of schools of thought before becoming committed to neoplatonism. In Athens he published a work of literary criticism showing his mastery of textual analysis, the so-called *Homeric Questions*. According to tradition, it was Longinus who "changed" the pupil's name from its Syrian form (Malkos = prince) to the Greek Porphyrios (= purple, the princely color). In 262 or 263, when he was about thirty, Porphyry committed himself to the neoplatonic school, having met Plotinus in Rome when the teacher was sixty. Assembled around the sage were the wealthy, the wise, and the merely curious of both sexes from Rome and far beyond. On arrival—and as an indication of his philosophically pre-cocious temperament—Porphyry sat down to write a treatise *against* Plotinus. After examining it, Plotinus assigned the task of refuation to his disciple Amelius. Porphyry's own description of this early "dispute" gives us some insight into the style of philosophical argument which, later and unsuccessfully, Christian teachers would apply to his writings:

I replied to what [Amelius] had written; Amelius answered my reply; and the third time with difficulty I understood the doctrine, changed my mind and wrote a recantation which I read in the meeting of the school. After this I believed in Plotinus' writings. (Porphyry, *Life of Plotinus*, trans. Armstrong, 18)

The process of disputation (propositions followed by refu-tation) was the Socratic means of arriving at truth. Christian work in the world. This was done through "upward striving," a diverting of the spiritual gaze away from the confusions of the changing world toward the unchanging perfection of the world of ideas. The task, however, was practical rather than mystical. It began with a clarification of everyday understanding ("What does Plato mean by 'an idea'?"). It included a correction of our desires, since the body is naturally attracted to the changeable, the material. It ended with a mastery of the process of dialectical philosophy as taught in the neoplatonic school.

The "end" of knowledge is truth, though one could also call it a "god." This "god" is not the Christian God, nor even the Christian *idea* of God. Theologians from the second century onward had misread Plato (and would later misread Plotinus and Porphyry) on this fundamental point. The confusion arises, as Étienne Gilson once noted, because "after so many years of Christian thought it has become exceedingly difficult for us to imagine a world where the gods are not the highest reality, while that which is the most supremely real in it is not a god" (E. Gilson, *God and Philosophy* [1941], p. 27). In Plato's mind, the gods were inferior to Ideas. The sun, for instance, was held by Plato—as by Constantine and the early church— to be a god. And yet in Plato's philosophy, the sun, who is a god, is a child of the Good, which is not a god. Gods were individual living beings, intelligible, necessary, and eternal (in the sense of being immortal: not-mortal), but they were not the immutable Ideas (cf. Plotinus, 6 *Ennead* 1.3).

Also unlike the Christian doctrine of God was Plotinus' understanding of the soul. A heavenly *eros* (attraction) dwells in every human soul—a natural but dysfunctional desire to move upward from stage to stage toward the perfection of Ideas and away from the imperfections that hem it in. The ascent makes the soul increasingly like a god—divine—in the sense that it increasingly loses the encroachments of mortality and becomes like the gods. This aim (ascent) is understood to be fundamentally practical, though the language in which it is expresed is that of Greek myth. The "upward ascent" is through *nous* or mind; the ascent, philosophically expressed, is the increase in understanding. Discursive thought leads to understanding: first of the intelligible, then of the divine, the original. By intuitive insight, the soul that has achieved this insight feels itself to be in union with the divine light but knows as well that it is only a part of this light. Individuation (and thus the Christian notion of a personal god-creator, resurrection of the flesh, and salvation of the individual soul) is the very opposite of this line of thought.

Plotinus' followers were fond of singing an ancient Greek song, still taught by the Stoic philosophers, about the beauty of this world. It was, after all, the launching point for the ascent of the mind to the realm of Ideas. Plotinus therefore insisted his students sing the song to defend his teaching against the barbarous idea of the Christians, that this world was a contemptible place—a view, oddly, which they had derived not from the Bible but from their own idiosyncratic interpretation of Plato (cf. 2 *Ennead* 3.5; 1.4; 3.9; 4.9, etc.).

While it is possible to overstate Porphyry's debt to Plotinus, the effect of the old teacher on the pupil seems to have approximated religious conversion. Porphyry recounts this in his *Life of Plotinus*. Whole families were attracted by his teaching. Women on their deathbeds gave their children into the keeping of the teacher, and he took numbers of children under his wing, serving collaterally as guardian, tutor in philosophy, and confidant. Plotinus won the trust of senators and politicans to such a degree that after twenty-six years of teaching in Rome—not the most charitable of cities—Plotinus was reckoned to have no enemies among the politicians of the city (*Life* 15; 9; cf. Eusebius, *Preparation of the Gospel* 10.3).

When Plotinus died after a long illness, Porphyry became head of the Roman school but was unable to ensure its survival. After a career in which he flirted with magic and tried to explain prophecy on philological grounds, he took on the task of explaining diversity in human perceptions of the divine. *Images of the Gods*, which has perished but is known to us through later citations, is an early work of demythologization within the pagan context. The gods are there viewed as symbols of the powers operating in and through nature. Zeus is regarded as the supreme power, the living essence of the universe, which writers incorporating sections of Porphyry's polemic were burned in order to eliminate what one critic, the bishop Apollinarius, called the "poison of his thought." Apollinarius' response to Porphyry amounted to thirty books. Methodius of Olympus (ca. 311), Eusebius, the church historian, and St. Jerome also turned their hand to answering the philosopher. Second, the ninety-seven fragments gathered by Harnack, half of which were taken from the fourth(?)-century writer Macarius Magnes, are enough—if barely enough—to give us the shape of Porphyry's critique. Harnack (*Porphyrius, gegen die Christen,* 1916) has been accused of giving too much weight to the words of the pagan philosopher cited by Macarius (who does not actually name his opponent as Porphyry), whose voice is muted by the agenda of the Christian teacher. In a study done some twenty years ago, Timothy Barnes argued that the fragments used by Macarius could not be used uncritically to reconstruct Porphyry's lost work. (cf. T. D. Barnes, 1973, pp. 424–42), and the tendency since that time has been to chip away at the number of "authentic" Porphyrian statements educible from Macarius' work (cf. R. L. Fox, 1986, p. 771 n.1). The dating of the fragments has proved to be an even more stubborn problematic.

For good or ill, however, the Macarius fragments must serve as a basis for any discussion of Porphyry's work, even though they represent a very shaky foundation (cf. Wilken, p. 136). Expressing qualified doubt about Macarius' use of Porphyry's books does not mean that he did not use them. On average, the voice to be heard is that of a conservative pagan intellectual arguing a line with unmistakable affinities to Porphyry's known criticisms of the Christian faith. If the voice seems hollow, more akin to Justin's fictional Trypho than to Origen's full-blooded Celsus, it is because Macarius is less respectful of his source. Conversely, there can be no doubt that the source is not merely fictional. The pagan's words are far too strong and too coherent to be attributed to a conglomerate of the Christian teacher's imagination. The philosophy is consistently that of a neoplatonist who finds Christian teaching objectionable on grounds we can trace directly to Porphyry's school and for which there are analogies in *Marcella,* the *Philosophy from Oracles,* and especially *On the Return of the Soul,* where moderate praise for the character of Jesus is coupled with scathing criticism of the disciples, especially Peter (a dabbler in the black arts).

That Macarius does not name his opponent and sometimes seems to characterize rather than quote his opinions could easily be explained as a strategic decision by a Christian teacher who wished his defense to survive. Naming his adversary— or quoting him too precisely—would have almost certainly guaranteed the burning of Macarius' defense (cf. Waelkens, 1974). Put appositely, anyone wishing to write a defense of the faith in the fourth or fifth century would have been foolhardy to identify the enemy as Porphyry. The persecutions were still a recent memory, and the role of pagan philosophers in promoting them could not be forgotten or forgiven. An inadequate defense would only serve to enshrine the words of the critic. Even Jerome was guilty, in his famous *Commentary on the Book of Daniel* (early 5th century) of suppressing Porphyry's comments when necessary to his defense (cf. *Commentary on Matthew* 24.16) as when he discusses the famous "prophecy" of the destruction of the temple in Dan. 9.24f.

In a devastating critique which has not survived, but which has evoked plenty of reaction from his critics, Porphyry began *Against the Christians* with an attack on the Christian view of prophecy. Although Platonism had actually inspired the allegorical interpretation of prophecy by teachers such as Origen, the philosopher's nemesis, Porphyry condemned the use of allegory as a means of explaining away difficulties and contradictions in the biblical text. It has even been suggested that Porphyry drew some of his polemic directly from Origen's book on the difficuties of interpreting scripture, the *Stromateis*. All he had to do was to "accept Origen's negative statements . . . and reject the deeper spiritual meanings" that Origen found for them (Grant, 1972, p. 292). Despite his contempt for allegory—a feature which shines through rather clearly in Macarius' fragments—the philosopher was more concerned with chronology than interpretation. He denied the extreme antiquity of the Moses story, the traditional dating of the law, and the ascription of the Book of Daniel to the period before the Babylonian captivity in the sixth century B.C.E.

persisted in building their houses of worship—sometimes in plain view of the imperial palace.

Porphyry was doubtless distressed by the failure of Rome to contain the spread of what he regarded as a dangerous superstition. Only a few decades later, Eusebius could boast not only of the spread of the gospel but of its infiltration into the highest circles (*Eccles. History* 8.1.1; 8.11.2)—precisely the success that Porphyry feared.

When he sat down to write his extensive refutation of Christian teaching, Porphyry was not starting from scratch. He had composed years before a book about the worship of the gods titled *Philosophy from Oracles*, in which he offered a reasoned defense of the old religions, while expressing a reserve bordering on contempt for popular expressions of religious devotion. As we have already noted in his mature work, the *Letter to Marcella*, Porphyry's attention was focused on a god who is incorporeal, immoveable and invisible—a "God concept," so to speak, who requires neither sacrifice nor prayer (cf. *Of Abstinence* 2.37) Like Platonists before him, Porphyry recognized the world as being full of lesser divinities and influences—gods and *daimones*. These lesser divinities were for *hoi polloi*, the man on the street and women in the marketplace. Thus in the *Philosophy from Oracles*, Porphyry assigns a place to the high god, to the Olympians, the celestial bodies, and in book three of the same work, a place to heroes (divine men), among whom he numbers Jesus.

Traditionally it has been thought that Porphyry began by thinking highly of Jesus but badly of his followers who had elevated him to divinity. The evidence is very thin and what exists is extremely obscure. It comes mainly from Augustine (see *City of God* 19.22-23), where Porphyry is said to have praised the Jews for their belief in one God but condemned the Christians for their worship of Jesus as a god. But on the analogy that great men, Heracles, Orpheus, and Pythagoras among them, are rightly worshiped as gods for their feats, it makes nonsense of the evidence to say that Porphyry thought highly of Jesus. In Book 19 of *City of God*, Augustine quotes Porphyry as saying in the *Philosophy from Oracles* that it is easier to fly through the air like a bird than to recall a superstitious Christian wife to her senses. Let her do what she pleases, he advises, "singing lamentations for a god [Jesus] who died in delusions, who was condemned by right-thinking judges, and killed in hideous fashion by the worst of deaths, a death [whereby he was] fastened by nails" (*City of God* 19.23). The conclusion can only be that the Christians mistakenly worship Jesus as a god, even though he is plainly not to be compared with the heroes. This, then, makes sense of Apollo's "oracle" to the effect that Christians cannot be persuaded of the foolishness of worshiping a criminal as a god—a theme recurrent in anti-Christian polemic from at least the time of Celsus and also in the critique of Macarius' pagan.

Bluntly put, Augustine's "defense" must be viewed with extreme caution. The notion that the gods have pronounced Jesus devout and the inclusion of Jesus among the "wise men of the Hebrews" (*City of God* 19.23) have all the flavor of Christian interpolation. In the same passage cited by Augustine, an oracle of Hecate seems to suggest that the soul of Jesus, though entangled in delusion and error, like other souls, was released from this error after death and entered, like the souls of other men, into heaven. It is this "soul" that the Christians "in their ignorance" mistakenly worship as God. This oracle is not, however, as so many have suggested, a favorable assessment of the person or teaching of Jesus. Furthermore, the sentence, "What I am about to say may appear startling to some: I mean that the gods have pronounced Christ to have been extremely devout, and have said that he has become immortal," makes no sense unless Augustine himself would have regarded it as startling coming from his patron philosopher. And it is more startling still that Porphyry should have introduced the oracle in this way. By the same token, we need not attribute its invention to Augustine, since Eusebius (*Demonstration* 3.6.39–3.7.1) has already cited the same passage to show that Porphyry did not despise Jesus, as Hierocles, a Christian-hater and pupil of Porphyry, apparently did. Subsequent references to the piety or to the wisdom of Jesus (cf. Augustine, *Harmony* 1.11) seem to refer to the single oracle of Hecate quoted by Augustine as belonging to Porphyry's work. Nevertheless, it cannot be maintained from this scant and internally improbable testimony that Christians feared Porphyry's work "because it gave a positive appraisal of Jesus within the framework of pagan religion" (Wilken, p. 160). Much less can it be maintained that statements derogatory to Jesus should not be attributed to Porphyry, or that Porphyry would have maintained a favorable view of Jesus on the basis of the latter's worship of the one God of the Jewish people. Augustine's comparison of the oracle of Apollo, which called Christ unrighteous, with that of Hecate, which called him "a man of supreme piety," is Augustine's attempt to show up contradictions in Porphyry's attack. In fact, however, Augustine repeatedly misrepresents the Hecate oracle, and progressively reinterprets its fundamentally negative assessment of Jesus' teaching.

By the same token, it is clear that Porphyry, like pagan obervers before him, believed that the disciples of Jesus departed from the founder's teaching; but it does not follow that he held to the view that Jesus himself taught a religion centering on the supreme God of all (cf. Wilken, p. 154). The truth seems to be that Porphyry regarded Jesus as a criminal, justly punished for his crimes by the power of the Roman state, and hence undeserving of the status of hero or of the divinity conferred upon him by his misguided followers.

Whatever Porphyry may have thought of Jesus, the bulk of his criticism was reserved for the evangelists, the apostles of Jesus—especially Peter—and the Christian mission epitomized by Paul. He began with the premise that the gospel accounts were not harmonious (Augustine, *Harmony* 1.1) and moved quickly to discuss specific cases, ranging from the words of Jesus on the cross to the healing miracles ascribed to him. Macarius' "pagan" deals with most of the same subjects we know, from Augustine's *Harmony*, to have attracted Porphyry's criticism: that the apostles fabricated genealogies, that there are discrepancies concerning the time of Jesus' death, that Jesus had not claimed to be divine, and that the teaching of Jesus was obscure and self-contradictory. Augustine's characterization is borne out by Jerome (*Epistle* 57), who records that Porphyry found the evangelists unable to produce a coherent chronology and frequently wrong in their use of Hebrew prophecy. Mark cites a passage from Malachi and attributes it to Isaiah (Mark 1.2); Matthew attributes to Isaiah a verse of Psalm 77, and so on.

A general view of Porphyry's work yields the following picture: Beginning with an introduction in which the ambitions of the Christians were repudiated ("they want riches and glory ... they are renegades seeking to take control": *Apoc.* II.7f.], Porphyry went on to show their unworthiness. They accepted but misunderstood the "myths" and oracles of the Jews, then turned around and altered these to make them even more contemptible (Harnack, *Frags.* 1, 52, 73). Their religion had neither a national anchor nor a rational basis; they required initiates to accept everything on blind faith. Moreover, the initiates themselves were the worst sort of people, moral invalids who (cf. Celsus) found security in their common weakness (*Frags.* 81, 82, 87). The Christians had proved that they cared nothing for those who had lived in the era before the coming of Jesus; these could not be saved.

The Christians taught absurd doctrines about the suffering of God or the suffering of a son of the supreme God. They also prayed for the destruction of the world—which they hated because they were hated by it—and believed that at its end they alone would be raised bodily from the dead (*Frags.* 84, 85, 89, 92, 94). The sky would be destroyed and the ruler of the world would be cast into an outer darkness, as a tyrant might be driven out by a good king. By such thinking the Christians showed contempt for God. How could God be angry? How, if all powerful, as even some of their teachers said, could his property have been stolen in the first place?

After attacking the chronology of the Old Testament (cf. *Frags.* 39; 40-41; 68; 43) and arguing against Christian allegorical interpretation, Porphyry took up the subject of the writers of the gospels and epistles, whom he regarded as ignorant, clumsy, and deceptive. The fact that he wages his assault chiefly against the "pillar" apostles, Peter and Paul, suggests that he regarded the destruction of their reputations essential to wiping out the claims of an emergent Catholic Christianity (*Frags.* 2-18, 49, 55, 19-37). Thus Paul himself had called Christian believers "wretches" (1 Cor. 6.9f.) and promised his followers the resuscitation of the "rotten, stinking corpses of men" (cf. Augustine, *City of God* 22.27). As for Peter, he had been called "satan" even by Jesus, yet was entrusted with the keys to the kingdom of heaven (*Apocriticus* III. 19f.]. The apostles proved themselves traitors, cowards, weakling and hypocrites—even in the accounts written by them.

The Jesus allegedly praised for piety and wisdom by Hecate in Porphyry's *Philosophy from Oracles,* finds no grace in *Against the Christians.* His parables are trivial and incomprehensible. They are "hidden from the wise but revealed to babes" (Matt. 11.25), a state of affairs which encourages ignorance and unreasonableness. Jesus and his followers represent a lethargic ethic of the status quo, the very opposite of the Greek quest for moral excellence; indeed, his blessing on the poor and downtrodden and his repudiation of the rich make moral effort impossible. Had he not taught that selling everything and giving it to the poor (Matt. 19.21), thereby becoming a lout and a beggar and a burden on others, was the height of Christian perfection? (*Frags.* 52, 54, 56, 58)

Furthermore, Jesus did not follow his own advice. His show of weakness in the Garden of Gethsemane prior to his arrest was disgraceful: having preached fearlessness in time of persecution to his disciples, he exhibited only fear and trembling at the moment of his capture. When Jesus stood before his accusers, he spoke like a guilty man, not like a hero on the order of Apollonius of Tyana who had been hauled before Domitian (*Frags.* 62, 63; cf. Philostratus, *Life of Apol.* 8.8f.). Had he been a god on the order of the ancient heroes, he would have flung himself from the parapet of the temple; he would have appeared after his death to haunt Herod and Pilate— or indeed, to the Senate and People of Rome, to prove he had risen from the dead. That would have convinced everyone of the truth of Christian belief, and it would have spared his followers the punishment they now suffered for their beliefs. In short, had Jesus cared for his followers he could have taken care to spare them their martyrdom.

References and Bibliography[*]

Andresen, C. *Logos und Nomos.* Berlin, 1955.
———. "Justin und der mittlere Platonismus." *ZNTW* 44 (1952): 157-95.
Armstrong, A. H. "Plotinus." In *Cambridge History of Later Greek and Early Mediaeval Philosophy,* pp. 195-210. New York: Cambridge University Press, 1967.
Arnobius. *Against the Pagans.*
Augustine. *Of the City of God against the Pagans.* Ed. J. E. C. Welldon, London, 1924.
Bardesanes, *Opera.* Ed. F. Nau. Paris, 1907.
Barnes, T. D. "Legislation against Christians." *Journal of Religious Studies* 58 (1968): 32-50.
———. "Porphyry Against the Christians: Date and Attribution of Fragments." *Journal of Theological Studies,* n.s. 24 (1973): 425-30 [a controversial redating of the Harnack fragments and attribution based on questionable premises].

---

*For Greek and Latin Christian sources refer to the Berlin Corpus, the Venice Corpus, *Corpus Christianorum* and Migne's Patrologies; useful selections are provided in J. Stevenson, *A New Eusebius: Documents Illustrative of the History of the Church to A.D. 337* (London, 1957; rev. ed., W. H. C. Frend, 1986). Short-title references in the text are to my translations of patristic sources available in these editions. In the case of ancient sources, as when a particular edition or translation has been used for critical reasons, a bibliographical annotation follows the listing.

Barnes, T. D. "Pre-Decian *Acta Martyrum.*" *JTS,* n.s. 19 (1968): 509–31.

Baynes, N. H. "The Great Persecution." In *Cambridge Ancient History,* vol. 12. Cambridge, 1964.

Benoit, A. "Le *contra Christianos* de Porphyre: ou en est la collecte des fragments." In *Paganisme, judaisme, christianisme: mélanges M. Simon,* pp. 263–70. Paris, 1978.

Bidez, J. *La vie de l'empereur Julien.* Paris, 1930.

———. *Vie de Porphyre.* Paris, 1913.

Blondel, C. *Macarii Magnetis quae supersunt ex inedito codice edidit.* Paris, 1876.

Braverman, J. *Jerome's Commentary on Daniel: A Study of Comparative Jewish-Christian Interpretation of the Hebrew Bible.* Washington, D.C., 1978.

Brown, P. *Society and the Holy in Late Antiquity.* Berkeley and Los Angeles: University of California Press, 1982.

———. "The Diffusion of Manichaeism in the Roman Empire." *JRS* 59 (1969): 92–103.

Cameron, A. "The Date of Porphyry's ΚΑΤΑ ΧΠΙΣΤΙΑΝΩΝ." *Cambridge Quarterly,* n.s. 17 (1967): 382–84.

Carrington, P. *The Primitive Christian Catechism.* Cambridge, 1950.

Casey, P. M. "Porphyry and the Origin of the Book of Daniel." *JTS,* n.s. 27 (1976): 15–33.

Chauvin, P. *A Chronicle of the Last Pagans.* Cambridge, Mass.: Harvard University Press, 1990.

Clarke, G. W. "Some Observations on the Persecution of Decius." *Antichton* 3 (1969): 63–76.

———. "Two Christians in the Familia Caesariis." *Harvard Theological Review* 64 (1971): 121–24.

Clement of Alexandria. *The Miscellanies* (ET [= English translation]: ANCL, Edinburgh, 1892).

Courcelle, P. "Antichristian Arguments and Christian Platonism from Arnobius to St. Ambrose." In *The Conflict between Paganism and Christianity in the Fourth Century,* ed. A. Momigliano, pp. 151–92. Oxford, 1963.

Crafer, T. W. *The Apocriticus of Macarius Magnes.* London, 1919.

Crafer, T. W. "The Work of Porphyry against the Christians and its Reconstruction." *JTS* 15 (1914): 59–60.

Croke, B. "Porphyry's Antichristian Chronology." *JTS* 34 (1983): 168–85.

Cyprian. *On the Lapsed and On the Faith of the Church Catholic.* Ed. M. Benevot. OECT, Oxford, 1971.

Danielou, J. *The Development of Christian Doctrine.* London, 1964.

Den Boer, W. "A Pagan Historian and His Enemies: Porphyry Against the Christians." In *Scriptorum paganorum* 1–4: *Saec. de Christiana Testimonia.* Leiden, 1948.

Dio Cassius. *Roman History.* Trans. E. Cary. Cambridge, Mass.: Library of Christian Classics, 1914.

Dodds, E. R. "Tradition and Achievement in the Philosophy of Plotinus." *JRS* 50 (1960): 1–7.

Duchesne, L. *De Macario Magnete et scriptis ejus.* Paris, 1877.

Eusebius, *Against Hierocles.* PG 22. 797–800; trans. F. Conybeare. Cambridge, Mass.: Harvard University Press, 1912.

———. *History of the Church.* Ed. Schwartz. Leipzig, 1903; trans. J. Oulton. Cambridge, Mass.: Harvard University Press, 1932.

———. *Life of Constantine.* Ed. J. Heikel, CGS 7. Leipzig, 1902, pp. 1–148.

Fox, R. L. *Pagans and Christians.* New York, 1987.

Frend, W. H. C. "The Persecutions. Some Links between Judaism and the Early Church." *Journal of Ecclesiastical History* 9 (1958): 141–58.

———. *The Rise of Christianity.* Philadelphia, 1987.

Geffcken, J. *The Last Days of Graeco-Roman Paganism.* Oxford, 1978.

Glover, T. R. *The Conflict of Religions in the Early Roman Empire.* New York, 1909.

Goppelt, L. *Christentum und Judentum in ersten und zweiten Jahrhunderten.* Gütersloh, 1954.

Grant, R. *The Letter and the Spirit.* London, 1957.

Grant, R. M. "Porphyry among the Early Christians." In *Romanitas et Christianitas,* ed. W. den Boer, pp. 181–88. Amsterdam/London, 1973.

———. *Early Christianity and Society.* New York, 1977.

Grant, R. M. *Eusebius as Church Historian.* New York, 1980.

Hanson, R. P. C. *Allegory and Event. A Study of the Sources and Significance of Origen's Interpretation of Scripture.* London, 1959.

Harnack, A. von. *The Mission and Expansion of Christianity in the First Three Centuries.* ET: London, 1908; rpt., 1963.

——. *Neue Fragmente des Werkes des Porphyrius gegen die Christen.* Berlin, 1921.

——. *Porphyrius gegen die Christen. 15 Bücher, Zeugnisse, Fragmente und Referate.* Berlin, 1916.

Heinemann, I. "The Attitude of the Ancient World toward Judaism." *Review of Religion* 4 (1940): 385–400.

Hinchliff, P. *Cyprian of Carthage and the Unity of the Christian Church.* London, 1974.

Hippolytus. *Commentary on Daniel* [CGS 1, Leipzig, 1897].

Hoffmann, R. J. *Celsus On the True Doctrine.* Oxford, 1987.

Inge, W. R. *The Philosophy of Plotinus.* London, 1929.

Jedin, H., and Dolan, J. P., eds. *From the Apostolic Community to Constantine.* New York, 1980.

Jerome. *Commentary on the Book of Daniel.*

Jones, A. H. M. *Constantine and the Conversion of Europe.* New York, 1949.

Justin Martyr. *1 Apology.* PG 6. 328–469; ET: C. Richardson, London, 1953.

——. *Dialogue with Trypho.* Ed. A. L. Williams. London, 1930.

Kelly, J. N. D. *Early Christian Doctrine.* Edinburgh, 1958.

Keresztes, C. "Two Edicts of the Emperor Valerian." *Vigiliae Christianae* 29 (1975): 81–95.

Kettler, F. H. "Origenes, Ammonius Sakkas und Porphyrius." In *Kerygma und Logos*, ed. A. Ritter, pp. 182–201. Göttingen, 1979.

Knipfling, J. R. *The Libelli of the Decian Persecution.* HTR 16 (1923): 345–90.

Kraeling, C. H. "The Christian Building." In *The Excavations at Dura Europas: Final Report* 8.2. New Haven, 1967.

Labriolle, P. *La réaction païenne.* Paris, 1934. [Viz., pp. 223–96.]

Lactantius. *Divine Institutes.* Ed. S. Brandt and G. Laubmann, CSEL 19, Vienna, 1890; ET: ANCL.

Lactantius. *On the Death of the Persecutors.* Ed. J. Moreau, *Sources chrétiennes,* 39. Paris, 1954.

Lebreton, J. "The Pagan Opposition." In *The History of the Primitive Church,* 1949.

Liebschultz, J. H. W. G. *Continuity and Change in Roman Religion.* Oxford, 1979.

Lietzmann, H. *From Constantine to Julian.* London, 1960.

Lilla, S. R. C. *Clement of Alexandria: A Study in Christian Platonism and Gnosticism.* New York, 1971.

Lloyd, A. C. "Porphyry and Iamblichus." In *The Cambridge History of Later Greek and Early Medieval Philosophy,* ed. A. H. Armstrong. Cambridge, 1967.

Lucian of Samosata. *On the Death of Peregrinus.* Trans. A. M. Harmon. Cambridge, Mass.: Harvard University Press, 1936.

MacMullen, R. *Constantine.* New York, 1969.

———. *Roman Social Relations, 50 B.C. to A.D. 284.* New Haven, 1974.

———. *Paganism in the Roman Empire.* New Haven, 1981.

Marcus Aurelius. *Ad se ipsum.* Ed. J. Dalfen. Leipzig, 1979.

Markus, R. A. *Christianity in the Roman World.* New York, 1964.

Meredith, A. "Porphyry and Julian Against the Christians." ANRW, ed. H. Temporini, 23/2, 1126–28. Berlin, 1980.

Minucius Felix. *Octavius* [ET: G. H. Randall. Cambridge, Mass.: Harvard University Press, 1931].

Momigliano, A. *Alien Wisdom, The Limits of Hellenization.* London, 1975.

Moreau, J. *Les persécutions du christianisme dans l'Empire romain.* Paris, 1956.

Nautin, P. *Lettres et écrivains chrétiens aux IIe et IIIe siècles.* Paris, 1962.

———. "Trois autres fragments de livre du Porphyre *Contre les Chrétiens.*" *Revue Biblique* 57 (1950): 409–16.

Neusner, J., ed. *Christianity and other Graeco-Roman Cults.* Leiden, 1974.

O'Meara, J. J. *Porphyry's Philosophy from Oracles in Augustine.* Paris, 1959.

Origen. *Against Celsus* [trans. of *Contra Celsum,* ed. and introd. H. Chadwick. Cambridge, 1953].

Origen. *Commentary on the Book of Matthew.*

———. *Commentary on St. John's Gospel* [ed. E. Preuschen. CGS 10: Leipzig, 1903].

———. *On First Principles* [ed. P. Koetschau; ET: G. Butterworth, New York, 1936].

Pelikan, J. *The Excellent Empire: The Fall of Rome and the Triumph of the Church.* San Francisco, 1987.

Peterson, E. *Der Monotheismus als politisches Problem.* Leipzig, 1935.

———. *Frühkirche, Judentum und Gnosis.* Freiburg, 1959.

Philostratus. *Life of Apollonius of Tyana* [ET: F. C. Conybeare. Cambridge, Mass.: Harvard University Press, 1932].

Plotinus. *Enneads.* 6 vols. Trans A. H. Armstrong. Cambridge, Mass.: Harvard University Press, 1966.

Porphyry. *Launching Points to the Realms of Mind.* Trans. K. S. Guthrie. Grand Rapids, 1986.

———. *Pros Markellan.* Ed. and trans. (German) W. Potscher. Leiden, 1969; ET: A. Zimmern, London, 1986.

Puech, H. C. *Le Manicheisme: son fondateur, sa doctrine.* Paris, 1949.

Quispel, G. "Christliche Gnosis und judische Heterodoxie." *Evan. Theologie* 14 (1954): 1–11.

Rudolph, K. *Gnosis: The Nature and History of Gnosticism.* San Francisco, 1983.

Rufinus. *Commentary on the Apostolic Creed.*

Schalckhauser, G. *Zu der Schriften des Makarios von Magnesia.* Leipzig, 1907.

Schmidt, K. L. *Le problème du christianisme primitif.* Paris, 1938.

Schoeps, H.-J. *Jewish Christianity: Factional Disputes in the Early Church.* Trans. D. Hare. Philadelphia, 1969.

Sherwin-White, A.-N. "The Early Persecutions and the Roman Law Again." *JTS,* n.s. 3 (1952): 199–213.

Simon, M. *Verus Israel.* Paris, 1948.

Socrates Scholasticus. *History of the Church.* Ed. R. Hussey. Oxford, 1853.

Sordi, Marta. *The Christians and the Roman Empire.* London, 1986.

Sozomen. *Ecclesiastical History.* Ed. J. Bidez CGS 50 (Berlin, 1960), ET: NPNF.

Ste. Croix, G. E. M. de. "Why Were the Early Christians Persecuted?" *Past and Present* 26 (1963): 6–38.

Syngrammata: Studies in Graeco Roman History. Ed. H. W. Pleket, pp. 167–77. Leiden, 1979.

Tertullian. *Against Marcion.* Trans. Evans, OECT, 2 vols. Oxford, 1972.

———. *Apology* [ET: T. R. Glover, Library of Christian Classics, Cambridge, Mass., 1931].

———. *Prescription against Heretics* [CSEL 70, 1–58].

Theodoret of Cyrrhus. *Summary of the History of Heresies* (PG 83, col. 335–556).

Walzer, R. *Galen on Jews and Christians.* Oxford, 1949.

———. "Porphyry and Arabic Tradition." *Fond. Hardt Entretiens* 12 (1966): 275–99.

Wilken, R. M. *The Christians as the Romans Saw Them.* New Haven, 1984.

Yadin, Y. *Bar Kochba, The Rediscovery of the Legendary Hero of the Second Jewish Revolt against Rome.* New York, 1971.